WOODCARVING
NOAH'S ARK

WOODCARVING
NOAH'S ARK

Carving and Painting Instructions for Noah, the Ark, and 14 Pairs of Animals

Shawn Cipa

FOX CHAPEL
PUBLISHING

© 2011 by Shawn Cipa and Fox Chapel Publishing Company, Inc., East Petersburg, PA.

Woodcarving Noah's Ark is an original work, first published in 2011 by Fox Chapel Publishing Company, Inc., East Petersburg, PA. No part of this book may be reproduced in any form or by any means, electronic or mechanical, without written permission from the publisher. The patterns contained herein are copyrighted by the author. Copies of these patterns may be made for personal use; however, they may not be duplicated for resale or distribution under any circumstances. Any such copying is a violation of copyright law.

Step-by-step photography provided by Shawn Cipa.

ISBN: 978-1-56523-477-2

Library of Congress Cataloging-in-Publication Data

Cipa, Shawn.
Woodcarving Noah's ark / Shawn Cipa.
    p. cm.
Includes index.
ISBN 978-1-56523-477-2
1. Wood-carving--Technique. 2. Wood-carving--Patterns. 3. Noah's ark in art. I. Title.
TT199.7.C565 2011
736'.4--dc22
                          2011003462

To learn more about the other great books from Fox Chapel Publishing, or to find a retailer near you,
call toll-free 800-457-9112 or visit us at *www.FoxChapelPublishing.com*.

Note to Authors: We are always looking for talented authors to write new books
in our area of woodworking, design, and related crafts. Please send a brief letter
describing your idea to Acquisition Editor, 1970 Broad Street, East Petersburg, PA 17520.

Printed in China
First printing: September 2011

ABOUT THE AUTHOR

Shawn Cipa began carving in 1993. Already possessing a solid background in art, it wasn't long before woodcarving became a driving passion in his life. He began by carving wood spirits and soon after tried his hand at Old Father Christmas. Although Shawn has carved many different subjects by commission, he admittedly prefers all things whimsical in nature. Walking sticks, canes, Santas, angels, and other mythical characters are just some of Shawn's repertoire.

Shawn Cipa

Shawn comes from an artistic family and has experience in several art forms, such as illustration, painting, and sculpture. Although working in most art mediums came easily to Shawn, carving wasn't one of them. Learning to sculpt by taking away rather than adding on, such as in clay sculpting, was a daunting task. However, perseverance paid off. Shawn's other skills include carpentry and photography. Shawn is also an accomplished musician of many years, a passion that rivals his love of the visual arts.

Shawn was recognized as a national winner in Woodcraft Supply Corporation's 2000 Santa Carving Contest. He is the author of *Carving Folk Art Figures*; *Woodcarving the Nativity*; *Carving Fantasy & Legend Figures in Wood*; and *Carving Gargoyles, Grotesques, and Other Creatures of Myth*. He has been featured in *Wood Spirits & Green Men* by Lora S. Irish and is a regular contributor of how-to articles to *Woodcarving Illustrated* magazine. Shawn does commission work from his Website and provides pieces to many collectors internationally. Shawn hopes to continue his carving endeavors with unending support from his family and friends, who have helped to encourage his efforts.

You can contact Shawn via his Website *www.shawnscarvings.com*.

Dedication

To my dear friends and family, members of Crossroads, and followers of Christ, thank you for your unending support. Also to my dear Trish, who has always supported me and encouraged me in my endeavors; her love is unconditional and pure. Thanks to God, who has blessed me with this gift of creation.

Acknowledgments

Thanks to the staff at Fox Chapel Publishing who have given me this opportunity. To my fans and readers who have encouraged me to write this book, thank you for your much appreciated words of praise.

CONTENTS

HOW TO USE
THIS BOOK

This book contains patterns and reference photographs to guide you through the carving and painting of Noah, his wife, the ark, and 15 animals to fill the ark. Start with Noah, the lion, and the ark—after you've gone step-by-step through their creation and painting, you're ready to move on to the menagerie of animal patterns. You could create all of the animal pairs, or you could select a smaller set to carve. You could even create other animals by adapting Shawn's patterns to extend your floating zoo. Be sure to read the Carving and Painting Basics in Appendix II if you need extra help getting started, and don't forget to flip to the interesting In the Beginning, a discussion of the various cultural flood tales throughout the world.

PEOPLE AND THE ARK

Noah
page 14

Noah's Wife
page 130

Ark
page 50

WILD ANIMALS

Lions
page 30

Bears
page 88

Elephants
page 110

Giraffes
page 124

BIRDS

Pelicans
page 94

Flamingoes
page 96

Toucans
page 98

Owls
page 100

Doves
page 102

FARM ANIMALS

Bull & Cow
page 104

House Cats
page 120

Pigs
page 134

Sheep
page 138

SEA CREATURES

Fish
page 116

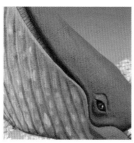

Whale
page 144

INTRODUCTION

...all the fountains of the great deep were broken up, and the windows of heaven were opened. And the rain was on the earth forty days and forty nights. ~ GENESIS 7:11-12 NKJV

The account of Noah, his ark, and the Great Flood is one of the most well-known and instantly recognizable Bible stories of the Old Testament's book of Genesis. It tells us of a time when the human race was so wicked and evil that God had become full of regret and decided to destroy all of creation. All, that is, with the exception of Noah and his family.

Noah was a simple and ordinary man, but he possessed one thing that separated him from every other living being on the planet: he had the grace and favor of God. In God's eyes, Noah was blameless and righteous, a lone island in a sea of evil and wickedness that was humankind.

As the story goes, God chose Noah to build an ark, a huge sea-worthy ship, the likes of which had never been seen or imagined before. Noah was commanded to take a sample of all living creatures—two of everything, male and female—on the ark with him.

God then let loose the flood waters that wiped out all living things. Approximately a year after the rain began to fall, the waters receded, the animals were set free, and life began anew.

I often imagine what it must have been like for Noah to have been chosen by God from among all of humanity to carry on our race. Imagine how hard he must have tried to reason with everyone he spoke to, hoping against hope that they would repent. Imagine his frustration when all the people ridiculed him while they watched him build his massive boat. Imagine the amazing experience of witnessing thousands upon thousands of animals approaching the ark, all docile and of their own accord. Imagine the absolute resolution felt when those very first drops of rain fell, confirming to Noah that everything God had said was really going to happen. Imagine the harrowing experience of surviving within the ark for those many months, tossing and churning about listlessly, trusting and waiting.

. . .

Noah's story is one of faith, commitment, obedience, catastrophe, adventure, and grace. It has shown me that I can trust my faith regardless of unforeseen or even incomprehensible circumstances, and that when the chips are down and all seems hopeless, the rain will come to an end. The clouds will part, and the sun will shine once more upon my face. This story reminds me there is always hope in the face of darkness.

Ever since I began to carve wood, I always wanted to create my own version of Noah's ark. Many times I have been inspired in the past and had several false starts; either I lost interest, was pulled away to another project, or simply found the size of the project to be daunting. What I was lacking was a clear plan. I would just start without direction, and inevitably the project would just fall apart and be forgotten, destined to sit upon one of my shelves among a graveyard of my many other unfinished misfits.

Finally, with the encouragement of my many readers (you know who you are) and with the support of Fox Chapel, I was granted renewed inspiration! I formulated a plan of attack and am very pleased to present to you my own folk art version of Noah's ark, complete with a sizable array of animal figures to be displayed as you please. Although most of the animals have a certain amount of detail and realism, I have attempted to infuse a "modern" folk art flavor by incorporating bold colors and my own stylization to the designs. The ark design itself is loosely based on those that were built in Germany in the nineteenth century as biblical teaching toys for children.

What can you, the reader and fellow carver, expect from this book? The carvings will appeal to

beginning and intermediate carvers alike. Most of the figure patterns are fairly simple and may be modified to accommodate a certain amount of detail, depending on your skill level. For example, you may choose to scroll saw the animals out of flat wood stock and leave them blocky, reflecting the more simple and traditional toy designs of the nineteenth century, or you may choose to carve them in the round, as I have done. You can omit more carving details and replace them with painted ones, or you can choose to add more carving detail than what I have shown. The overall scale of the figures is fairly small and could not be made much bigger without building an ark that would take up half the room for display! Of course, you may alter the scale as you wish, but remember that the smaller the figures get, the more fragile many details become and the more difficult they are to carve. This project also takes advantage of all those small scrap pieces of wood stock that you found too painful to discard.

The construction of the ark may be something new to some of you, and admittedly it does not utilize many carving skills; it is not unlike building a dollhouse. However, it does provide a great lesson in simple construction and will require certain tools to complete. Although I have strived to create this ark design to be as beginner friendly as possible and with readily available

materials, you may still need to alter the details to make the best use of your tools and skills.

Considering the many pieces and involvement required, the overall project would make a great joint effort for your local carving club or a group of carving friends. Perhaps someone in your group is more advanced at construction and can build the ark while others tackle the figure carving. This project is a great way to share skills and tools while strengthening the bond of friendship through collective creative efforts.

It is my sincerest hope that the average carver will find something new in these lessons, or perhaps maybe just something familiar and enjoyable, like an old warm blanket. Whichever is the case, please have fun, be safe, and start creating!

— Shawn Cipa

PART I
STEP-BY-STEP PROJECTS

I've designed two of these three step-by-step projects—Noah and the lion—to showcase the different skills you'll need to carve each of the animals in the final section of this book. The third project—the ark—involves woodworking skills that will be used only in that project.

Read through all the instructions and study the photographs first before you begin your project. Start with the patterns, work your way through the carving instructions, take a break, and then continue with the painting instructions. When you're finished you'll have the first two carvings and an ark to place them on.

CARVING AND PAINTING
NOAH

According to the Bible, Noah was the only man left in his generation that still followed God amidst a world of total wickedness and evil. Noah was already an old man by the time God instructed him to start building the ark—about 480 years old! Scholars suggest that it could have taken Noah and his sons up to 120 years to build the massive ship. Can you imagine being wholly committed to any one project that long? This obedient act of Noah took more time to accomplish than the longest life span of anyone today. Perhaps this is one great challenge his story gives to us: to live a life of commitment and obedience to those ideals that are most important to us. By the time the floodwaters were let loose, Noah was 600 years old. He lived to be 950 years old, the third oldest person ever.

This design of Noah obviously marks him as an old man, staff in hand. I have given him an arms-outstretched position as if to say, "Look what I have done with the Lord's help and guidance! Come aboard, the rains are coming!" His shape is simple and very easy to band saw. You will need to implement basic carving techniques, such as whittling, stop cutting, and chip carving. You will also need to use V-tools and various gouges to create texture. This carving also requires simple assembly skills (the walking staff). The design elements of Noah that you learn in this lesson will help you to complete Noah's wife as well.

Your beginning block will need to measure 5" (127mm) high by 4" (102mm) wide, with a thickness of 1½" (38mm). Because this project is small, you will only need to saw the front pattern image. Although a bit of clamping will be needed, most of the work can be done in a handheld position. For the walking staff, I suggest using a stronger wood than basswood, such as black walnut, so it won't be as fragile on such a small scale. The blank must measure ⅜" (10mm) by ¼" (6mm) by 4" (102mm) long. The top of the staff is larger, while the shaft itself will be whittled down to about ⅛" (3mm) to fit in the drilled hole of Noah's enclosed fist.

This is a fun and simple project; however, because of the small scale, care must be taken when carving the details in the face and hands. Take your time and have fun!

Front

Drill
⅛" Hole

Grain

Back

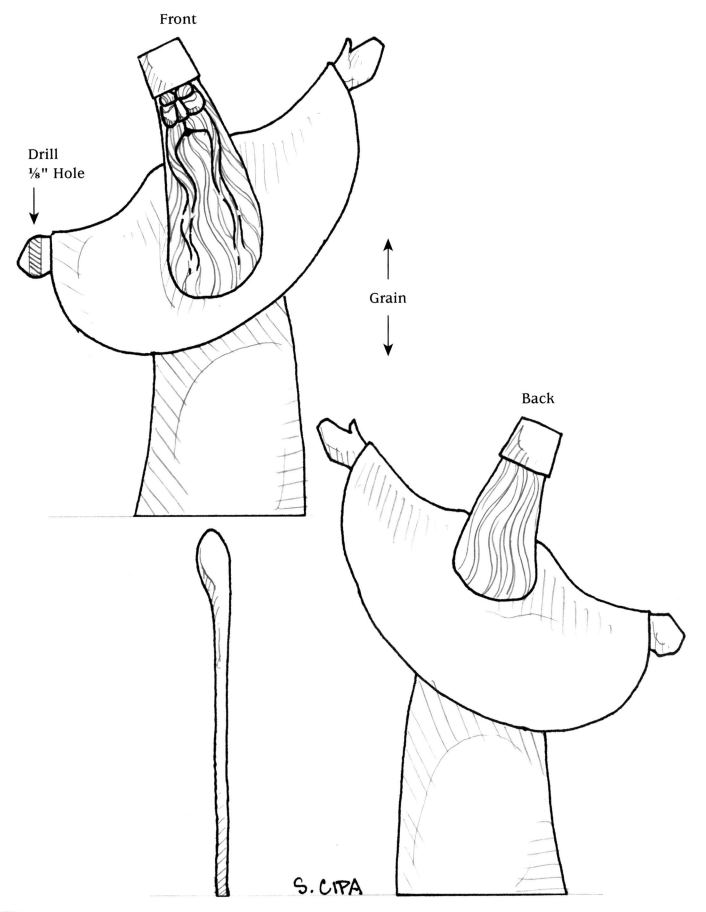

S. CIPA

PHOTOCOPY AT 100%

Front

Left Side

Right Side

Back

Top

CARVING

Tools and Materials: Carving

- › Basswood block 4" x 5" x 1½" (102mm x 127mm x 38mm)
- › Hardwood ⅜" x ¼" x 4" (10mm x 6mm x 102mm), for the staff
- › Standard carving knife
- › Spear point carving knife (or a knife with curved edge)
- › Small-bladed detail carving knife
- › 1" (25mm) shallow gouge
- › 1" (25mm) bent shallow gouge (optional)
- › ⅜" (10mm) palm V-tool
- › ½" (13mm) shallow fishtail palm gouge (optional)
- › ½" (13mm) half-round palm gouge
- › ⅛" (3mm) palm V-tool
- › ½" (13mm) macaroni tool (optional)
- › Band saw
- › Hand drill or handheld power drill
- › ⅛" (3mm) drill bit
- › Pencil
- › Cyanoacrylate adhesive

1. BAND SAW THE BLANK. Using the pattern on page 16, band saw the blank from 1½" (38mm)-thick stock.

2. TAPER THE FRONT. Secure the blank in a vise with the front of the piece facing up. Using a 1" (25mm) shallow gouge, begin to taper the blank from the bottom to the top. Reduce the thickness toward the top by about half, leaving the bottom at full thickness.

3. TAPER THE BACK. Flip the piece over, and repeat the tapering again. Do not cut as deep. The top should be no less than ½" (13mm) thick; the bottom should stay as close to the original thickness as possible.

4. THIN THE ARMS. Turn the piece to the front again. Using a bent shallow gouge, thin each arm extension while leaving a raised hump in the main body. At the same time, round the bottom edges a bit. **Note: A straight gouge could also be used here.**

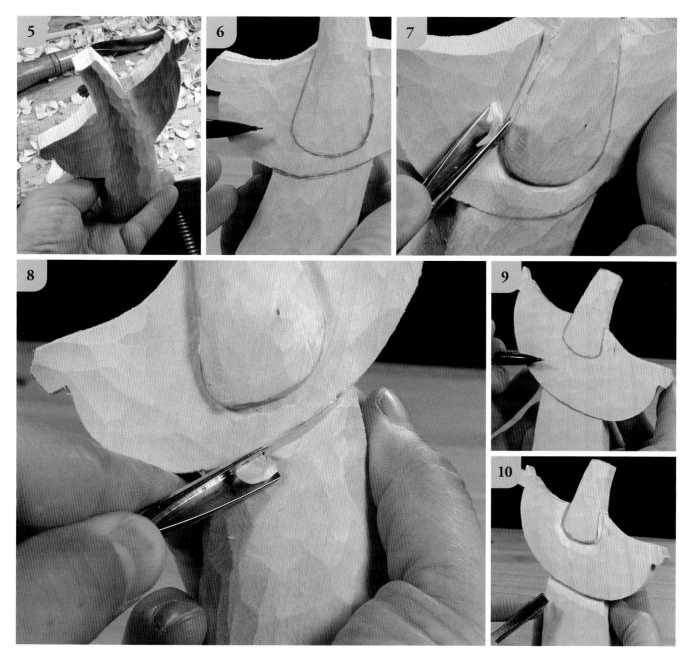

5. RESULTS. Note how the shadow accentuates the contour of the center hump.

6. DRAW THE BEARD. From this point, you will no longer need the vise. Hold the piece carefully while you carve. Use a pencil to draw Noah's beard and the bottom edge of his shawl.

7. OUTLINE THE BEARD. Using a ⅜" (10mm) V-tool, define the beard. Keep it shallow at the bottom, going deeper up toward the shoulders. Be sure to tilt the flat side of the V-tool toward the body when cutting so that the beard stands forward.

8. OUTLINE THE SHAWL. Using the ⅜" (10mm) V-tool, define the shawl in the same manner as the beard, tilting the flat of the tool toward the lower portion.

9. TURN TO THE BACK. Turn the piece to the back, and draw lines for Noah's hair (not as long as his beard) and the bottom edge of the shawl, as shown.

10. OUTLINE. Using the ⅜" (10mm) V-tool, define the hair and shawl.

CARVING

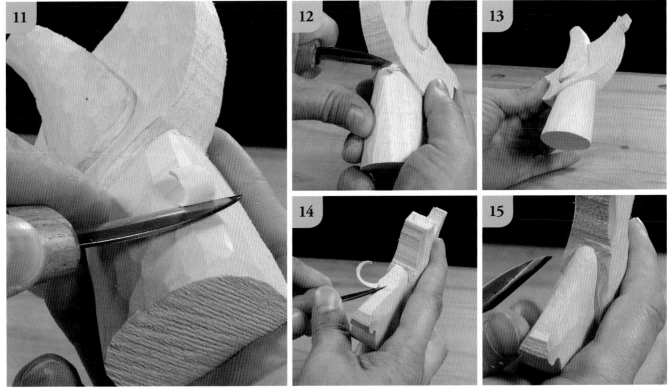

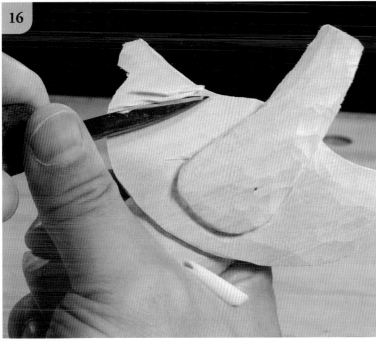

11. SHAPE THE LOWER ROBE. Using a standard carving knife, begin to round and shape the lower robe area below the shawl.

12. CONTINUE TOWARD THE BACK. Make stop cuts under the shawl, then work toward those to round the robe below the shawl.

13. RESULT. The bottom robe is completely shaped; notice how the very bottom of the carving is now an oval shape.

14. ROUND THE ARMS. Using the knife, begin to round the hard edges on the top of Noah's outstretched arms. I am working on his right arm here.

15. ROUND THE SHOULDERS. Using the knife, round the shoulders where they meet the head section. Do this using stop cuts and whittle the area to shape. I finished the right shoulder here; do the left shoulder as well.

16. SHAPE THE SHAWL. Using a spear-point knife, begin to thin and shape Noah's outstretched shawl by shaving off slices from the surface. The spear-point blade allows me to create a concave surface effect. Carve the front.

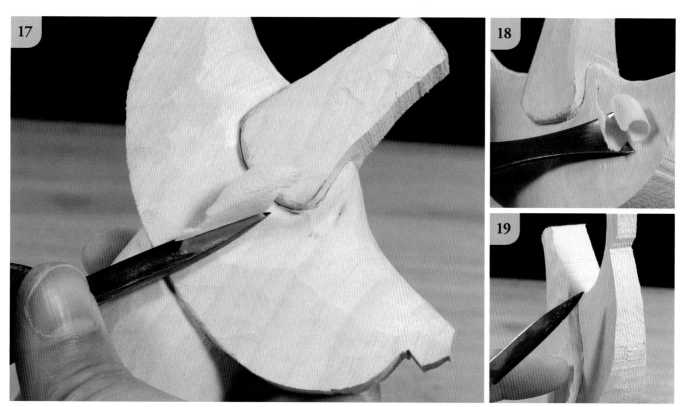

17. SHAPE THE SLEEVES. Continue on the back, shaping the top of the sleeves and the area below his hair.

18. THIN WITH A GOUGE. A shallow gouge can help to thin out these areas where the knife may be awkward. Here I am using a ½" (13mm) shallow fishtail palm gouge.

19. RESULT. Notice how the upper left arm is much thinner at the top. Both arms should be similar in shape and size.

20. CARVE THE HAND. Using the standard knife, begin to separate Noah's left hand from his shawl. Do this by making stop cuts, then carefully slicing away thin bits of the hand. Repeat this process on the back.

21. SHAPE THE HAND. Carefully round and shape the left hand, still using the standard knife. The hand has become thin and somewhat fragile now, so carve with small, controlled cuts.

22. RESULT. Notice that it appears to extend out from within the shawl. The hand and thumb have been rounded to shape as well.

CARVING

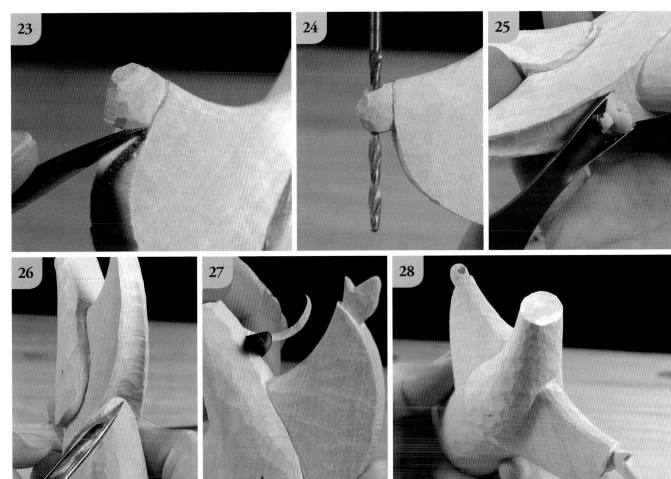

23. CARVE THE RIGHT HAND. Still using the standard knife, begin to separate Noah's right hand from his shawl in the same manner as his right with one exception: because this hand is fisted and will be holding a walking staff, keep it considerably thicker to accommodate the drilled hole in the next step.

24. DRILL A HOLE. After rounding the fist, carefully drill a hole for Noah's staff. Hold the figure upright on a flat surface. Using a ⅛" (3mm) drill bit, bore a hole through the fist from top to bottom and perpendicular to the flat supporting surface, as shown.

25. FINE TUNE THE SHAWL. Using a ½" (13mm) half-round palm gouge, slightly hollow the underside of Noah's outstretched shawl-covered arms. Be sure not to cut into the very outside edges; if you do, you will mar the rounded swoop of the shawl's lower edge.

26. RESULT. The underside of the upper left arm is completed. Use a spear point knife to clean up the hollowed area where it meets the hand and the body. Do the other arm.

27. ROUND THE HEAD. Using the standard knife, begin to round Noah's head into a slightly tapered cylindrical shape. Shape the beard and hair. Round off the hard edges of the beard and hair.

28. RESULT. The head portion is fully shaped. Notice that the top of Noah's head is flat and circular. This circle should be no less than ½" (13mm) in diameter.

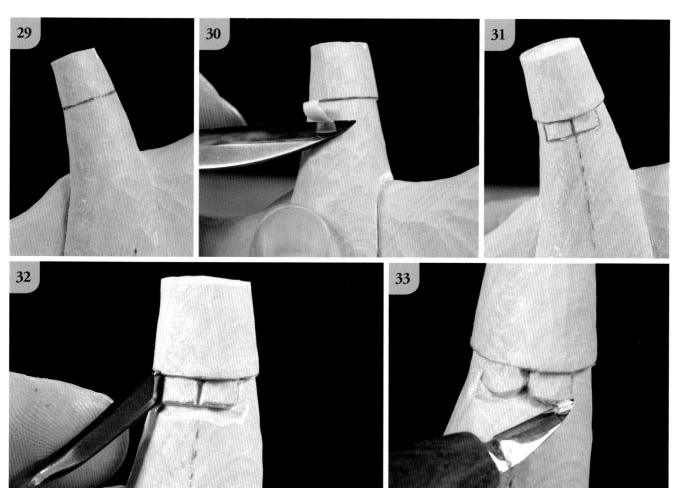

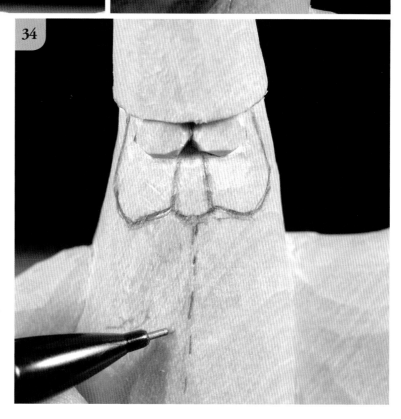

29. START THE HAT. Measure ½" (13mm) down from the top of Noah's head, and draw a line all the way around to mark the bottom of his fez-type hat.

30. CARVE THE HAT. Using the standard knife, create a stop cut along the hat line. Begin to taper Noah's head up to the stop cut all the way around, no more than ⅟₃₂" (1mm) deep.

31. DRAW THE EYEBROWS. Find the center of Noah's face, and draw rectangular eyebrows right under the brim of his hat.

32. CARVE THE EYEBROWS. Using a ⅛" (3mm) V-tool, define the eyebrows by carving a trench along the lines. Divide them through the center as well.

33. SHAPE THE EYEBROWS. Using a small detail knife, smooth out the V-tool marks on the face and shape the eyebrows by knocking off the hard corners.

34. DRAW FACIAL FEATURES. Draw in the nose and cheek lines, as shown.

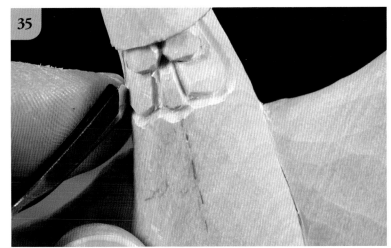

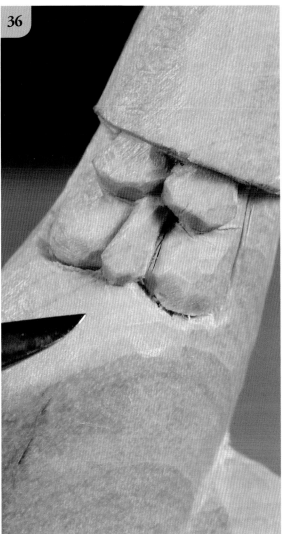

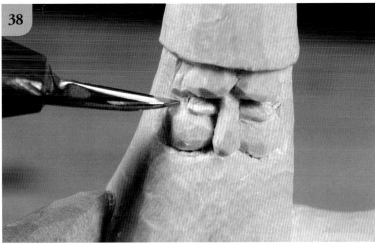

35. CARVE THE FACE. Using the ⅛" (3mm) V-tool, define the nose and cheeks by carving a trench along the lines, as shown.

36. DEFINE THE FACE. Using the detail knife, further define the face by shaping and rounding the cheeks and nose.

37. CARVE THE EYES. Create "squinty" eyes for Noah by removing a tiny horizontal sliver under each eyebrow with the detail knife.

38. DETAIL THE EYES. Add bags under Noah's eyes by using chip cutting techniques with the detail knife. Be very careful; you are working on a considerably small scale.

CARVING

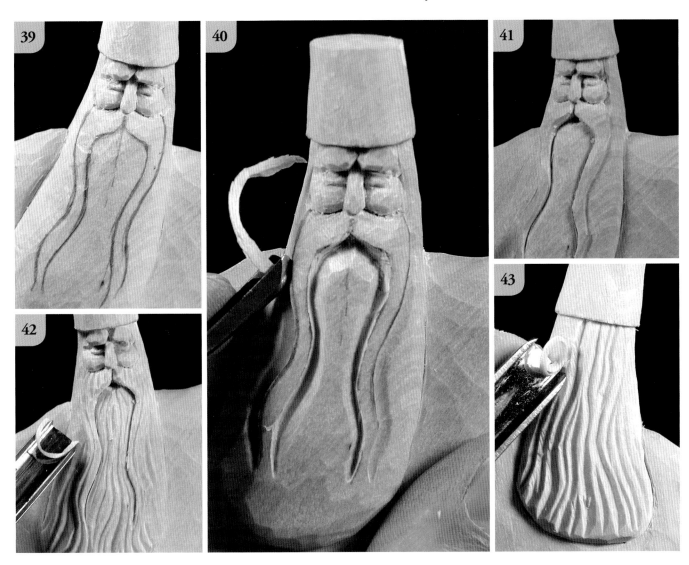

39. DRAW THE MUSTACHE. Draw Noah's mustache, as shown.

40. CARVE THE MUSTACHE. Using the ⅛" (3mm) V-tool, define the mustache by carving along the lines, as shown.

41. DETAIL THE MUSTACHE. Switching to the detail knife, clean up the mustache and remove a chip at the center to form Noah's mouth.

42. TEXTURE THE BEARD. Texture Noah's beard by incising intersecting wavy grooves using either a V-tool or macaroni tool. Here I am using a ½" (13mm) macaroni tool, which creates a more flowing groove than a V-tool.

43. TEXTURE THE HAIR. On the back side, texture Noah's hair in the same manner.

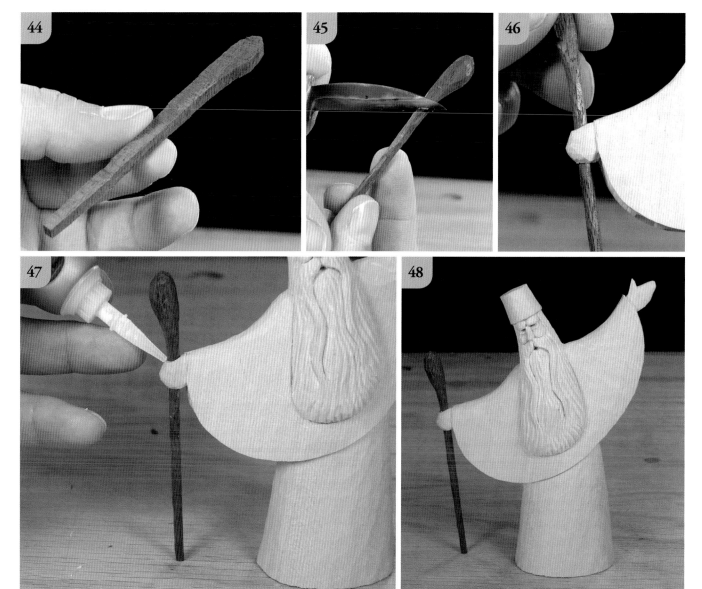

44. SAW THE STAFF. To create Noah's walking staff, band saw a blank according to the pattern on page 16. Since this piece will be quite small and potentially fragile, use a more durable wood than basswood. I chose black walnut. Cherry or oak is also a good choice.

45. SHAPE THE STAFF. Whittle the stick into shape, checking often to see how it fits into the drilled hole of Noah's right hand.

46. FIT THE STAFF. When Noah is standing on a flat surface, the finished staff should fit snugly in his hand and the bottom should rest on the surface. Do not force the staff into his fist, or you will risk splitting the hand apart. If the fit is too tight, whittle away a little more wood.

47. GLUE THE STAFF IN PLACE. Use a few drops of cyanoacrylate adhesive to glue the staff into the fist. Let the glue dry for an hour.

48. THE FINISHED CARVING. Noah is complete and ready for painting.

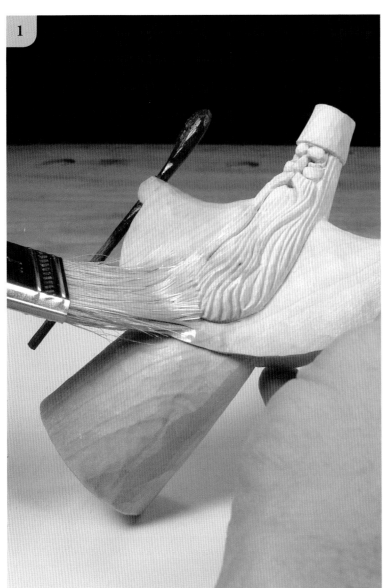

PAINTING

1. APPLY A LINSEED OIL MIX. Using a 1" (25mm) general purpose staining brush, slather the carving with a 50/50 mix of boiled linseed oil and mineral spirits. Let it dry for at least an hour. Wipe off any excess with a clean cotton rag.

2. PAINT THE ROBE. Using a ½" (13mm) flat brush, apply Snow White to Noah's lower robe.

3. PAINT THE UNDERSIDE OF THE SHAWL. Using a ¼" (6mm) round brush, apply a thin coat of Light Blue under Noah's shawl. Blend it out into the white. Apply this color all the way around.

4. PAINT THE SHAWL. Using the ½" (13mm) flat brush, apply Lilac Dust to Noah's shawl, front and back.

Tools and Materials: Painting and Finishing

- › ½" (13mm) flat brush for large areas
- › ¼" (6mm) round brush for smaller areas
- › ⅛" (3mm) round detail brush
- › 1" (25mm) general purpose staining brush
- › Fast drying satin polyurethane
- › Brown gel wood stain
- › Cotton rag
- › Boiled linseed oil
- › Mineral spirits

Paint Colors

- › Snow White / Americana
- › Light Blue / FolkArt
- › Lilac Dust / Apple Barrel Colors
- › Royal Purple / Americana
- › Antique White / Delta Ceramcoat
- › Slate Blue / FolkArt
- › Wedgewood Blue / Americana
- › Raw Sienna / FolkArt
- › Primary Red / Americana

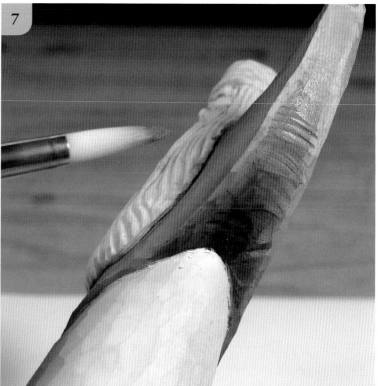

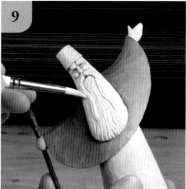

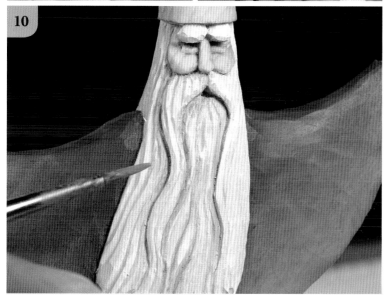

5. ADD MORE COLOR TO THE SHAWL. Use the ¼" (6mm) round brush to paint the underside and edges of the shawl, as shown.

6. PAINT THE TOP OF THE SHAWL. Using the ¼" (6mm) round brush, apply a thin coat of Royal Purple at the top of Noah's shawl and blend it out into the lilac color as you work down. Apply Royal Purple in this manner all the way around the top of his shawl.

7. APPLY MORE COLOR. Under the sleeves, use the ¼" (6mm) round brush to apply Royal Purple heavier close to Noah's body. Blend it lighter as you go out toward the hand.

8. RESULT. Notice how the colors work together to color Noah's robe and shawl.

9. PAINT THE HAIR. Using the ¼" (6mm) round brush, apply Antique White to Noah's beard and hair, front and back. Don't forget the eyebrows.

10. ADD COLOR TO THE BEARD. Using a ⅛" (3mm) detail brush, apply thinned out accent coats of Slate Blue to Noah's beard. Apply the color sparingly to the deepest areas in order to achieve a low light effect. Be sure to blend it out.

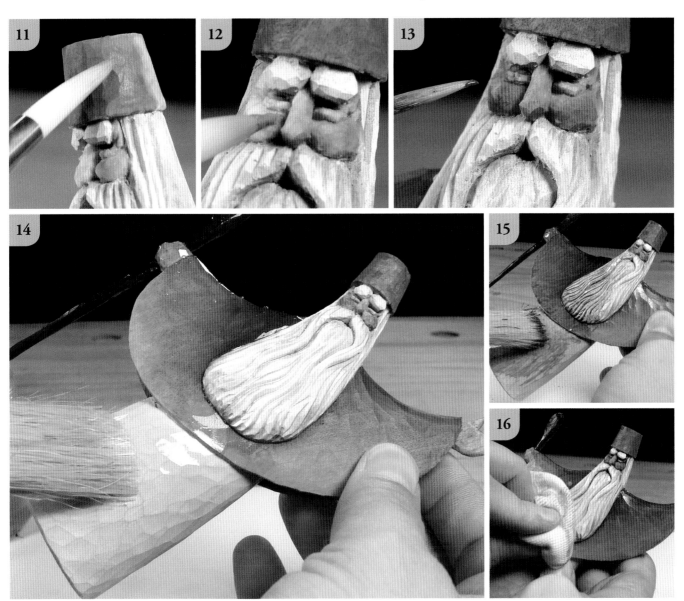

11. PAINT THE HAT. Using the ¼" (6mm) round brush, apply Wedgewood Blue to Noah's hat.

12. PAINT THE FACE. Using the ¼" (6mm) round brush, apply a wash of Raw Sienna to Noah's face and hands, giving him a tanned skin effect.

13. ADD COLOR TO THE FACE. Using the ⅛" (3mm) detail brush, blend a tiny bit of thinned out primary red to Noah's cheeks and to the tip of the nose; be sure to blend it in well. This coloring will give him a rosy-faced look.

14. APPLY SATIN POLYURETHANE. Allow the paint to dry for 1 hour, then use a 1" (25mm) general purpose staining brush to apply a very thin coat of satin polyurethane to Noah's entire body. Scrub it into each nook thoroughly. The finish will go on shiny, but if you apply it thin enough, it will dry almost matte. Let the piece dry overnight.

15. APPLY GEL WOOD STAIN. Using the same brush, apply a brown gel wood stain. Slather it on, working it into the nooks.

16. REMOVE ANY EXCESS STAIN. Immediately wipe off the excess with a clean cotton rag. Let the carving dry overnight before handling it.

CARVING AND PAINTING
THE LION

The lion, king of the beasts, is noble, brave, and fierce. He has long been a favorite Heraldic animal, adorning the family shields of royalty.

In Medieval times, it was believed the lion had three main natures: it erased its tracks with its tail when hunted, it always slept with its eyes open, and its cubs were born dead but were brought to life on the third day when the mother breathed in their faces or the father roared over them. In Christian allegory, these three natures had moral meanings. The lion erasing its tracks with its tail represented the way Christ concealed his divinity, only revealing himself to his followers. The lion sleeping with its eyes open again represented Christ, physically dead after crucifixion but still spiritually alive in his divine nature. The lion roaring over his dead cubs to bring them to life represented how God the father woke the son Jesus after three days in the tomb.

This design depicts our lion in full stride. His shape is moderately complex and will require a bit of finesse when band sawing around the legs; be sure to leave a little extra material. You will need to implement basic carving techniques, such as whittling, stop cutting, and chip carving. You will also need to use V-tools and various gouges to rough out and to create texture. The design elements you learn in this lesson will help you to complete the other four-legged animal projects in this book as well.

Your beginning block before sawing will need to measure 3½" (89mm) high by 6½" (165 mm) wide, with a thickness of 1½" (38mm). Because this project is small and only 1½" (38mm) thick, you will only need to saw the side pattern image. It is important that the grain runs vertically through the legs so they remain strong.

The waste material between the tail and the body of the lion can be largely removed ahead of time by drilling it out; however, this removal can be done by hand. Although a bit of clamping will be needed for the roughing out stage, most of the work can be done in a handheld position.

The tail in its finished state is fairly fragile due to the very short cross grain areas at the base and where it joins the rear leg. Great care should be taken when shaping it. If you happen to snap it, don't panic. Simply glue it back together with cyanoacrylate adhesive and move on.

Right Side

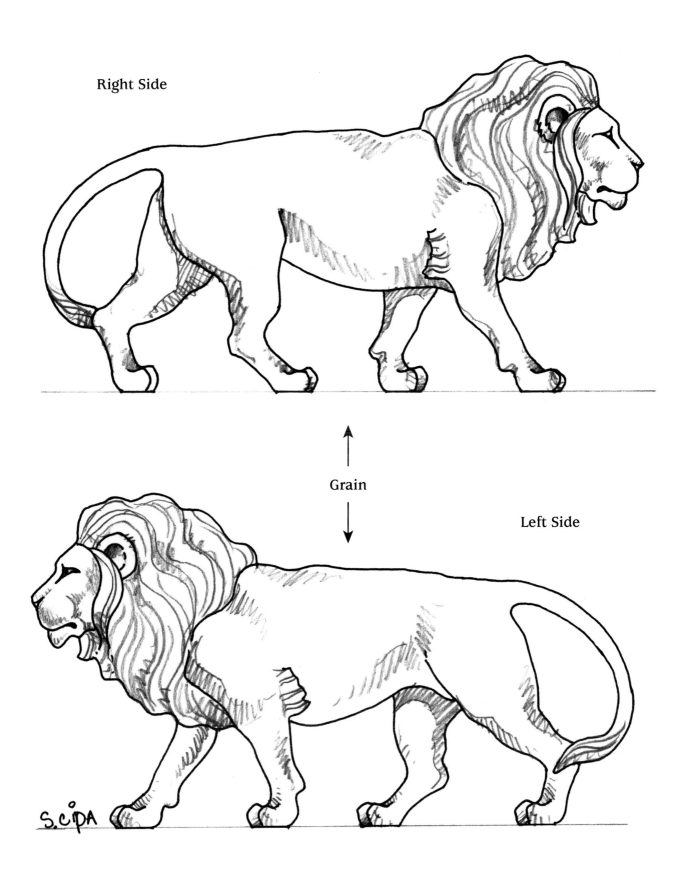

Grain

Left Side

PHOTOCOPY AT 100%

Left Side

Front

Back

Right Side

Top

The tail is very delicate.

THE LIONESS

The design of the lioness mimics the lion's position, but I've changed some of the anatomical elements a bit: obviously the mane is absent; she is a bit sway-backed; the belly hangs a little more (childbirth will do that); her hips sit a little higher, as do her shoulder blades; and I have placed her tail in a different position. Otherwise, the carving tasks remain very similar, as do the colors when painting.

Your beginning block before sawing will need to measure 3" (76mm) high by 6¼" (159mm) wide, with a thickness of 1½" (38mm). Because this project is small, you will only need to saw the provided side pattern image. As with the lion, it is important that the grain runs vertically through the legs so they remain strong.

Left Side

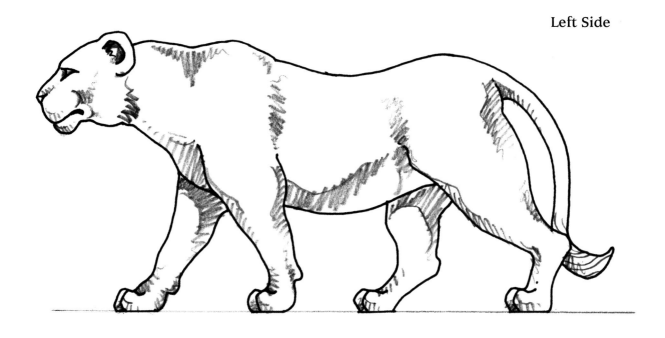

Grain

Right Side

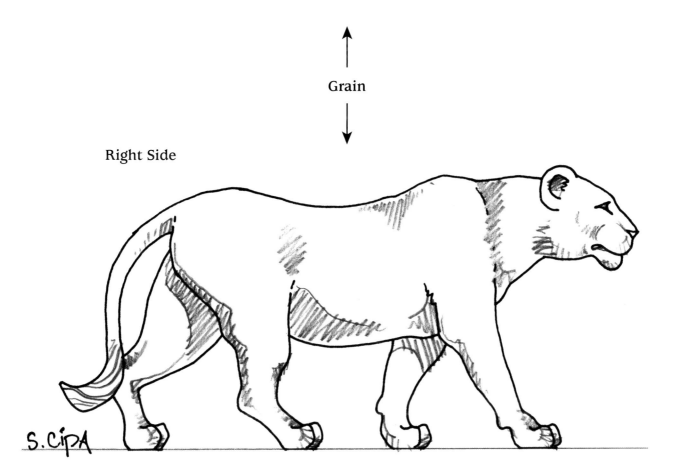

S. CipA

PHOTOCOPY AT 100%

Front

Left Side

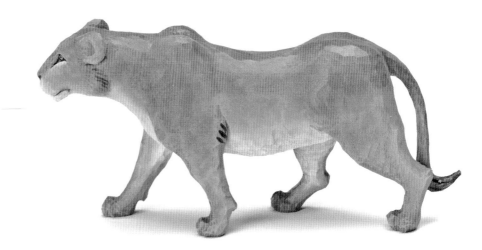

Back

Right Side

Top

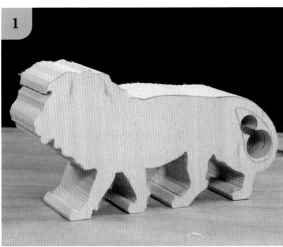

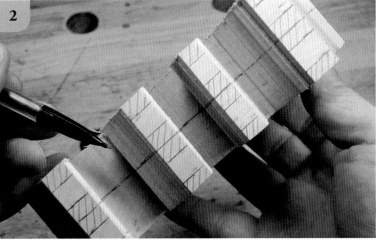

1. BAND SAW THE BLANK. Band saw the blank according to the pattern on page 32. Drill out the area between the tail and the rear to aid in removing waste; I used a ¾" (19mm) and a ½" (13mm) drill bit.

2. MARK THE FEET. Measure and mark the centerline all the way around the blank. Using this line as a reference, mark the lion's foot positions: measure ⅜" (10mm) out from the centerline on each side and another ⅜" (10mm) in from the edge to show the width of the paws.

3. DRAW THE PROFILE. On the top, loosely sketch the general contour of the lion's body profile. Make the torso area more narrow than the mane/head and the hips flair out slightly.

4. DRAW THE TAIL. Notice that the tail comes straight down from the middle and swings off toward the lion's rear left leg (rear view).

Tools and Materials: Carving

> Basswood block (lion) 3½" x 6½" x 1½" thick (89mm x 165 mm x 38mm)
> Basswood block (lioness) 3" x 6¼" x 1½" (76mm x 159mm x 38mm)
> Standard carving knife
> Spear point carving knife (or knife with curved edge)
> Small-bladed detail carving knife
> ⅝" (16mm) bent shallow gouge
> 1" (25mm) shallow gouge
> ½" (13mm) V-tool
> ⅜" (10mm) palm V-tool
> 3⁄16" (5mm) veiner
> ¼" (6mm) veiner
> Band saw
> Handheld power drill (optional)
> ¾" (19mm) and ½" (13mm) drill bits (optional)
> Pencil

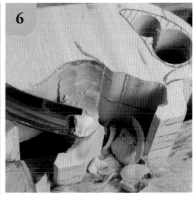

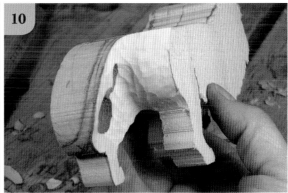

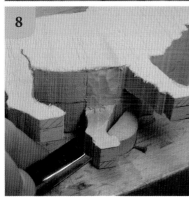

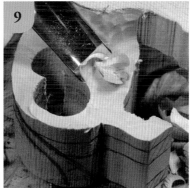

5. MARK WOOD TO REMOVE. Starting with the lion's left side, mark the right leg waste areas to be removed, as shown.

6. REMOVE WOOD FROM THE REAR LEG. Put the blank in a vise, left side up. Using a ⅝" (16mm) bent shallow gouge, start to remove the right leg waste. I chose a bent gouge because it eases wood removal in this tight area. As you go deeper, be sure to maintain the profile of the underbelly. Go all the way down to the rear right foot mark.

7. REMOVE WOOD FROM THE FRONT LEG. Do the same for the front right leg, as shown.

8. REPEAT ON THE OTHER SIDE. Flip the piece over, right side up, and repeat steps 5 to 7 to remove the left leg waste. The front leg is complete.

9. REMOVE WOOD FROM THE TAIL. When removing the rear left leg waste, also remove the tail waste down to the rear left foot mark.

10. RESULT. Notice how the tail swoops off to the left.

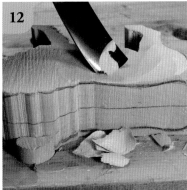

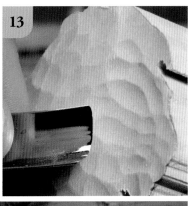

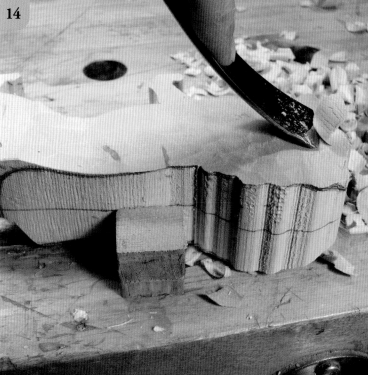

11. RESULT. All 4 legs are blocked out.

12. CARVE THE RIGHT SIDE. Using a 1" (25mm) shallow gouge, start to shape the overall body using the contour lines drawn in step 3 as a guideline. Work on the lion's right side first.

13. CARVE THE LION'S FACE. Switching to the ⅝" (16mm) bent shallow gouge, narrow the lion's face and muzzle area. Pull the piece out of the vise to check your progress.

14. CARVE THE LEFT SIDE. Flip the piece over and work on the lion's left side. Carve the torso and head area first with the ⅝" (16mm) bent shallow gouge, then use the 1" (25mm) shallow gouge to shape the body.

15. PROGRESS SO FAR. Notice that the left side tail area remains untouched.

16. REMOVE WOOD FROM THE TAIL. Still working on the left side, clear out the remaining waste wood within the inner tail void. First use the ⅝" (16mm) bent shallow gouge.

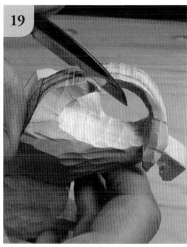

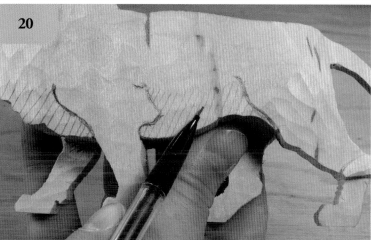

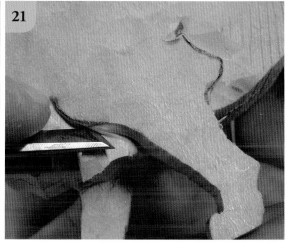

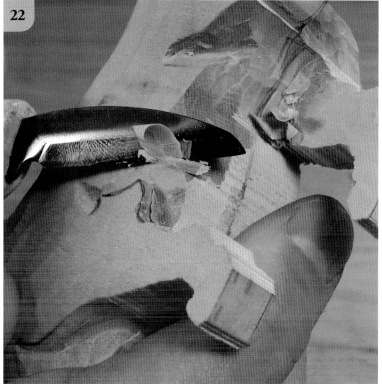

17. REMOVE WOOD FROM THE BASE OF THE TAIL. Finish up under the base of the tail with a ½" (13mm) V-tool.

18. DEFINE THE TAIL. Continue using the ½" (13mm) V-tool to define the tip of the tail where it overlaps the left rear foot.

19. CONTINUE TO DEFINE THE TAIL. You can now retire the vise and begin to carve the lion in a hand-held fashion. Using a standard carving knife, carefully remove any remaining waste from the left side of the tail area.

20. DRAW THE LEGS. Referring to the pattern, draw the left legs where they overlap the torso, as shown.

21. OUTLINE THE LEGS. Using a ⅜" (10mm) V-tool, define the legs by trenching around the drawn lines.

22. ROUND THE BELLY. With a standard carving knife, further define the separation of the legs and the torso. At the same time, round the belly.

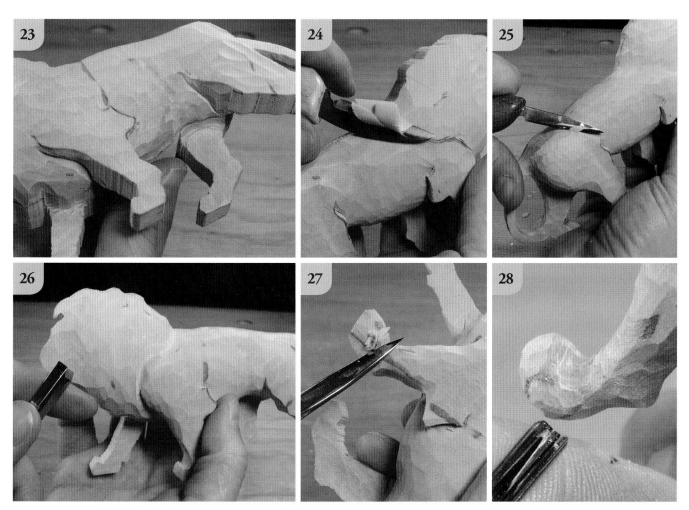

23. PROGRESS SO FAR. The lion's left underside is rounded all the way to the centerline. Notice that the area under the mane is also rounded. Repeat steps 20 to 22 to complete the right side in the same manner.

24. ROUND THE BODY. Using the standard carving knife, begin to round off the top edges of the lion's overall body. Work on both sides together to get a nice shape.

25. SHAPE THE SHOULDER BLADES AND HIPS. Scoop out a bit more wood around the shoulder blades and hips to make them more prominent. I switched to a spear point knife to make the task easier.

26. OUTLINE THE MANE. Using the ⅜" (10mm) V-tool, separate the lion's mane from the shoulder area. Refer to the pattern for placement of the v-groove, and complete both sides.

27. SHAPE THE FRONT LEGS. Using the spear point knife, start shaping the front legs and paws. The spear point will be more effective in achieving the various contours in these areas.

28. DEFINE THE TOES. In this close-up of the left front leg, notice how the muscle tone is loosely defined: the "wrist" is narrowed, and the paw is rounded. Use a 3/16" (5mm) veiner to scoop out the hollow on top of the paw and to define the toes.

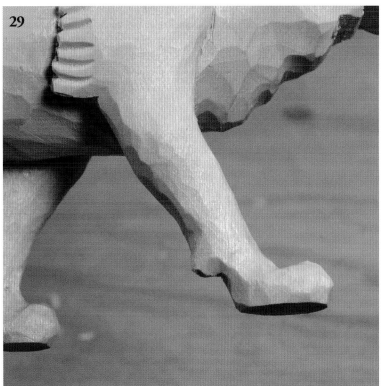

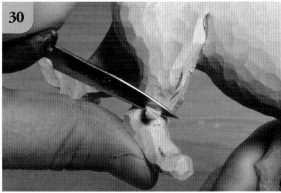

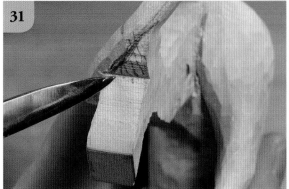

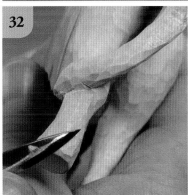

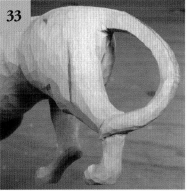

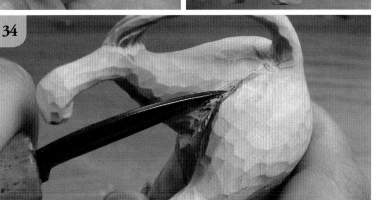

CARVING

29. CARVE THE TUFTS. The front legs are shaped to completion. I added the small v-cuts that will become the lion's elbow tufts.

30. SHAPE THE REAR RIGHT LEG. Shape the rear right leg with the spear point knife.

31. CLEAN UP THE AREA WHERE THE LEG AND TAIL MEET. Before shaping the rear left leg, this area where the tail connects to the leg must be addressed. Take out small bites with the spear point knife.

32. PROGRESS SO FAR. Continue to shape the rear left leg.

33. THE REAR LEFT LEG IS COMPLETE. Now round the tail carefully with the spear point knife. Remember, because of the grain direction, the tail could be fragile—and even more so depending on how brittle your wood stock is.

34. DEFINE THE HAUNCHES. Using the standard knife, define the rear haunches.

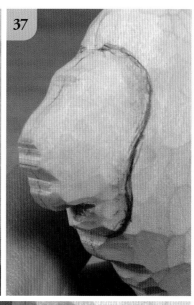

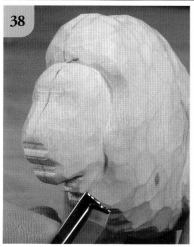

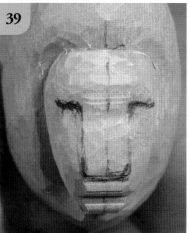

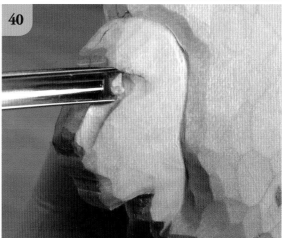

35. RESULT. The body and legs are now complete.

36. ROUND THE FACE. Using the spear point knife, round off the hard corners of the face and muzzle while still maintaining the profile.

37. DRAW GUIDELINES FOR THE MANE. Referring to the pattern, draw guidelines showing where the mane starts to grow out from the face. Mark both sides.

38. OUTLINE THE MANE. Using the ⅜" (10mm) V-tool, separate the face from the mane, shaping the mane with the flat side of the tool as you go along. Go all the way around.

39. DRAW THE NOSE. Redraw the centerline. Then draw the shape of the nose bridge and the brow; keep the nose wide.

40. DEFINE THE NOSE. Using the ³⁄₁₆" (5mm) veiner, define the nose bridge and eye sockets by running a trench along the outside of each guideline.

CARVING

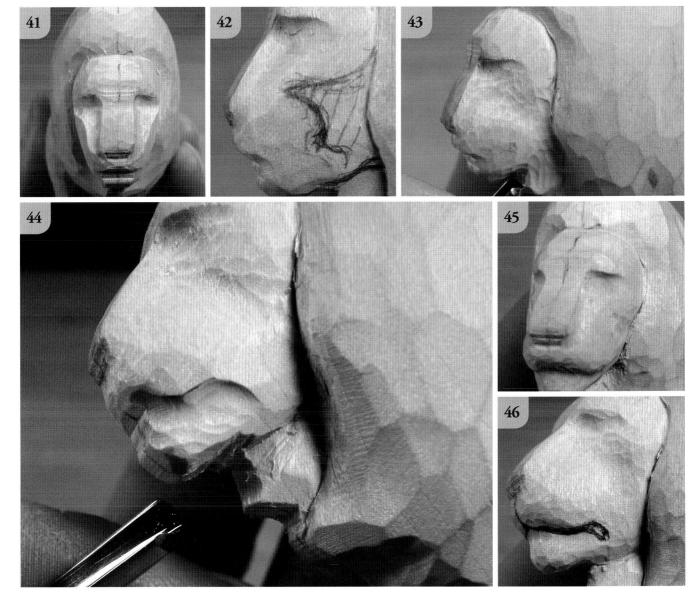

41. **RESULT.** Notice how the two sides of the face are symmetrical and evenly balanced.

42. **DRAW GUIDELINES FOR THE FACE.** Draw a guideline to define the cheek bone and the puffy upper lip (the whisker ball) of the lion.

43. **CONTINUE TO CARVE THE FACE.** Using the ³⁄₁₆" (5mm) veiner, hollow out the marked area by taking small bits at a time until you are satisfied with the results. Do both sides.

44. **DEFINE THE CHIN AND MOUTH.** Still using the ³⁄₁₆" (5mm) veiner, define the chin and mouth area by trenching along the lip line, as shown. The corner of the mouth drops off sharply at the end. Also separate the lower jaw from the beard, or small tuft of fur, underneath. A knife can help define this area. Do both sides.

45. **PROGRESS.** Smooth and clean up the veiner cuts with the tip of the spear point knife. Make sure all the main components of the face are defined: nose bridge, eye sockets, cheek bones, upper lip, and jaw.

46. **DRAW THE MOUTH.** Move on to the details that will bring the lion to life. Draw in the mouth on both sides, as shown.

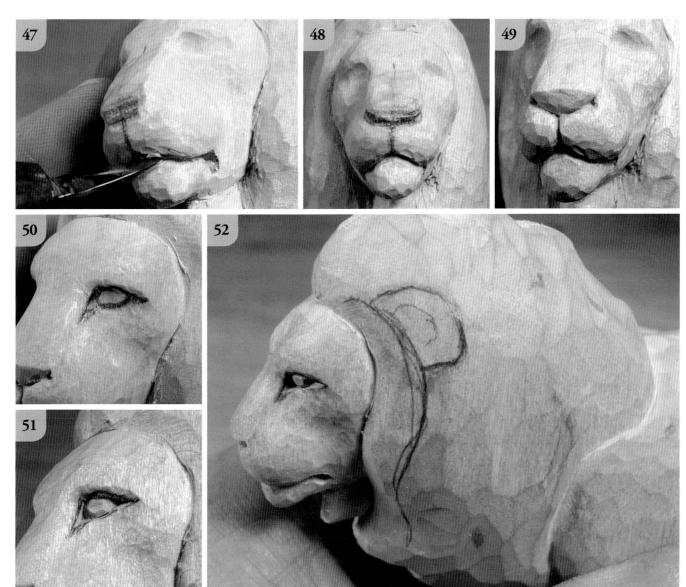

CARVING

47. CARVE THE MOUTH. Using a detail knife, define the mouth by plunge cutting and removing a small sliver of material all the way around.

48. DRAW THE UPPER LIP. The mouth is defined. Draw the nose and upper lip division.

49. CARVE THE UPPER LIP. Using the detail knife, define the nose and upper lip area. Notice that a small chip cut was removed to form a slight opening of the mouth. The muzzle is complete.

50. DRAW THE EYE. Draw in the eye as a triangular wedge and semi-circle within, as shown.

51. CARVE THE EYE. Using the detail knife, define the eye by removing small triangular chips, one on each side of the pupil. Complete the other eye in the same manner. This is small work, so make sure your knife is very sharp at the tip and take your time.

52. DRAW THE EAR. Draw in the ear, as shown. It appears to emerge from behind a lock of mane that drapes down and frames the lion's face.

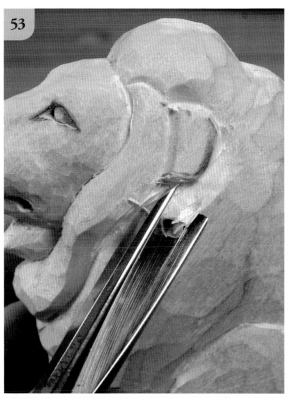

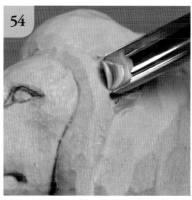

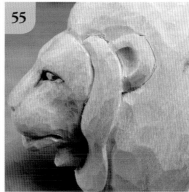

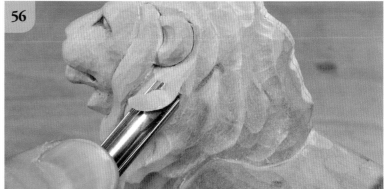

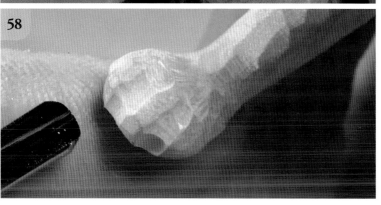

53. OUTLINE THE EAR. Using the ⅜" (10mm) V-tool, define the lock of mane and the ear by carving a trench around them.

54. CARVE THE EAR. Using a ¼" (6mm) veiner, hollow out the ear.

55. CARVE THE OTHER EAR. Clean up and define the ear area with a knife. I also cut back some extra material on the mane behind the ear. Complete the other ear in the same manner.

56. TEXTURE THE MANE. Using the ¼" (6mm) veiner, texture the mane by trenching out flowing channels, suggesting direction and movement in the mane's hair.

57. ADD MORE TEXTURE. Go back over the channels with the ⅜" (10mm) V-tool and further texture the mane by creating flowing, intersecting lines.

58. NOTCH THE PAWS. Using the ³⁄₁₆" (5mm) veiner, notch each paw with 3 notches each, to suggest the space between the toes. The lion is ready for painting and finishing.

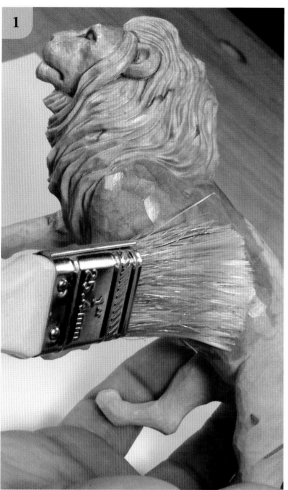

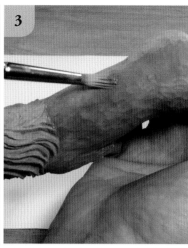

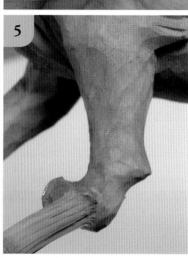

1. APPLY A LINSEED OIL MIX. Using a 1" (25mm) general purpose staining brush, slather the carving with a 50/50 mix of boiled linseed oil and mineral spirits. Let it dry for at least 1 hour. Wipe off any excess with a cotton cloth.

2. PAINT THE BODY. Using a ½" (13mm) flat brush, apply Antique Gold to the lion's entire body.

3. PAINT THE BACK. Switching to a ¼" (6mm) round brush, apply a thin coat of Raw Sienna to the lion's entire back, blending it down into the background color on the sides.

4. PAINT THE FOREHEAD. Blend in Raw Sienna on the lion's forehead and down the snout, as shown.

5. PAINT THE FEET. Blend in a bit of Raw Sienna on the tops of the paws and a little bit up each foreleg.

Tools and Materials: Painting and Finishing

> ½" (13mm) flat brush, for large areas
> ¼" (6mm) round brush, for smaller areas
> Fine detail brush
> 1" (25mm) general purpose staining brush
> Fast drying satin polyurethane
> Brown gel wood stain
> Cotton rag
> Boiled linseed oil
> Mineral spirits

Paint Colors

> Antique Gold / Americana
> Raw Sienna / FolkArt
> Antique White / Delta Ceramcoat
> Dark Chocolate / Americana
> Black / Americana
> Hauser Light Green / Americana

PAINTING

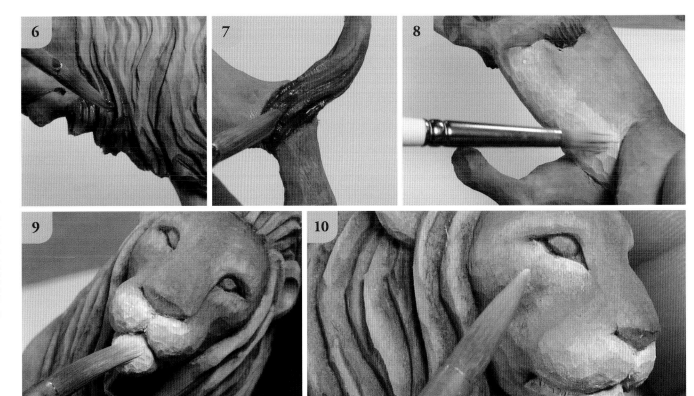

Note the details on the mane, ears, and face.

6. PAINT THE MANE. Still using the ¼" (6mm) round brush, sparingly apply a bit of Dark Chocolate to the mane. Apply it heavier toward the bottom, as if the lion's mane has been darkened on the ends by being dragged across the ground. Also apply a bit in the deepest grooves of the mane throughout.

7. PAINT THE TIP OF THE TAIL. With the ¼" (6mm) round brush, darken the tip of the tail with Dark Chocolate. Also apply a small amount of Dark Chocolate to the elbow tufts.

8. PAINT THE BELLY. Still using the ¼" (6mm) round brush, apply Antique White to the underbelly, painting the color heavier toward the center and fading into the background color toward the edges. Also treat the inside of each leg with a bit of white.

9. PAINT THE FACE. Apply Antique White to each whisker ball and the chin, as shown. Carefully blend out the edges.

10. BLEND COLOR UNDER THE EYES. Apply just a tiny bit of Antique White with the ¼" (6mm) round right under each eye opening, and blend the color outward.

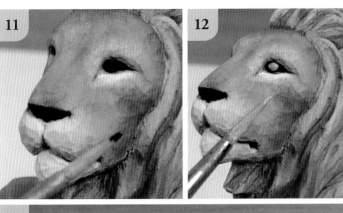

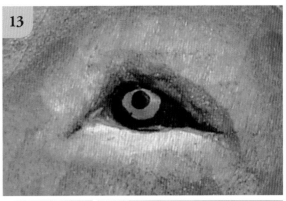

11. PAINT THE NOSE AND EYES. Using a fine detail brush, apply black to the nose and the entire eyeball of each eye; be careful not to touch the edges of the eye opening.

12. PAINT THE IRIS. Still using the fine detail brush, apply a small dot of Hauser Light Green for the iris. Be sure that the green dot floats within the black (the black should be visible all the way around the dot).

13. ADD THE PUPIL. Once the green is dry, carefully apply an even smaller dot to the center of the green to serve as the pupil; be sure that this dot floats within the green.

14. APPLY SATIN POLYURETHANE. After the paint has dried for at least 1 hour, apply a very thin coat of satin polyurethane to the lion's entire body, using the 1" (25mm) general purpose staining brush. Be sure to scrub it into each nook thoroughly. Watch the colors pop out as you do this step. The stain will go on shiny, but if you apply it thin enough, it will dry almost matte. Let the carving dry overnight.

15. APPLY GEL WOOD STAIN. Using the same brush, apply a brown gel wood stain. Slather it on, working it into the nooks.

16. WIPE OFF EXCESS STAIN. Immediately wipe off the excess with a clean cotton rag. Let the carving dry overnight before handling it.

CONSTRUCTING
THE ARK

I wanted to accomplish several points when designing this ark: an authentic folk art look and feel, an ark that could be partially disassembled for practical purposes, and a plan that could be accomplished by an amateur with basic tools and common store-bought materials.

The Design

When I finally chose my design—after many sketches—I calculated all the required measurements and built a half-scale model out of foam core board and hot glue. This action allowed me to see what the ark would look like in three-dimensions without committing to a full-blown project. Then I made adjustments to the design. For example, I originally had the arched areas of the cabin about 2" (51mm) higher than the final design; it looked good on a paper but was just too out of proportion at a larger scale. Also, the original window openings were square and crosshatched; I decided this idea looked too much like a barn and went with the round porthole instead. Finally, I originally designed the cupola as a traditional square style; again, this increased the barn effect, so I decided to go with a lathe-turned finial.

My design is based loosely on nineteenth-century German toy arks where the hull is basically a rectangular box with an angled bow and stern feature; I elaborated a bit by adding curved bowsprit pieces on each end for more interest and also to break up the overall hard-cornered look. They also double as a convenient way to pick up the entire ark, if needed. The cabin is houselike, except that I chose an open arched effect instead of doorways in order to open up more deck space for figure display.

Technical Design Features

My design requires absolutely no mitered corner cuts; every joint is a blunt union. I chose this feature to simplify the construction process and to cut down on the need for specialized tools.

I designed the ark to be built with readily available materials found at your local home improvement chain store, hardware store, and craft store. I even went with using premeasured, planed stock found right on the shelf. This usage will minimize the need to sand; however, some sanding will be required.

I made several cosmetic changes to this prototype of the ark before I settled on the final design presented here.

The painting and finishing have no special requirements; you will use the same products for the ark that you use for the carvings.

Explanation of Materials

The cabin section of the ark, as well as the deck, is primarily constructed of ½" (13mm) poplar stock, which is readily available off the shelf. The home improvement chain store lumber sections usually carry the same sizes in oak and white pine; you may choose the oak, but it is more expensive and would be a shame to paint. The white pine may also be used, but it is not as strong. I went middle of the road and chose the poplar. The widest stock available is 6" (152mm), which is actually only 5½" (140mm) wide, and comes in various lengths; you will need three 4' (1,219mm) long by 6" (152mm) wide pieces. Two will be laminated together, edge to edge, to get the required width for the cabin side panels and the deck. Because the width is actually 5½" (140mm), your total laminated width will be 11" (279mm), the measurement on which I based the cabin.

The roof panels of the cabin are ¼" (6mm) poplar stock and can be bought wherever you purchased the ½" (13mm) poplar stock. You will need one 3" (76mm) long by 6" (152mm) wide piece. Leftover pieces will be used for the ramp, the deck locks, and the weathervane (see page 55).

The cupola consists of two components: a basswood cube measuring 2½" (64mm) all the way around for the base and a store-bought, lathed-turned decorative finial. Finials can also be purchased at the home improvement center in the trim and molding section. Several options are available, so even though you may not find one exactly like mine, I'm sure you will have something equally attractive.

You will need approximately 50" (1,270mm) of ½" (13mm) square poplar dowel rod; it is sold in a maximum length of 48" (1,219mm), so you will need to buy an additional shorter piece. The dowel will serve as the ledge trim on the cabin and the peak trim on the roof. Another piece will be needed to serve as the stopper for the ramp.

Four pieces of small ⅛" (3mm)-thick trim measuring 4" (102mm) long and ⅜" (10mm) wide will be needed for the roof fascia; I found basswood trim at the local craft store in the wood section. Because these are such small pieces, you could actually cut them to size from larger stock if you wish.

The shingles I used were designed for dollhouse construction and can be found at a craft supply store. These particular shingles are cut from cedar and have an irregular shape, like miniature cedar shakes. You could easily make your own from any type of wood by simply using your band saw to slice thin strips from a ¾" (19mm)-thick board and then chopping them into 1" (25mm)-long pieces. You could also choose to omit the shingles and paint the roof instead.

As a decorative embellishment, I purchased miniature dental molding from the craft store, also found in the wood section. You may not find exactly the style that I used, but with quite a few choices, you'll be able to pick something that you find attractive. You will need an approximate length of 51" (1,295mm) for use on both the cabin and the hull sections.

The panels comprising the hull are all constructed from ¾" (19mm)-thick laminated pine and can be found in the lumber section of the home improvement center. This type of board has been laminated from much smaller pieces then planed and packaged. It is labeled "project board" and is intended to serve as small table tops, simple furniture, and so on. I prefer this wood for the hull because the lamination makes it strong and impervious to warping. The laminated sections also lend an aesthetic look. It comes 2' (305mm) wide and in various lengths; you will need a piece measuring 4' (1,219mm) long.

Finally, you'll need 1" (25mm)-thick basswood stock for the bowsprit pieces. I chose basswood because of the texture carving we'll be doing on these pieces. Each piece measures 11" (279mm) by 5" (127mm). You will need two.

Small holes drilled in the peak of the ark fit the wire that holds the birds in place.

Explanation of Tools and Construction

MEASURING. For general measuring, you'll need a yardstick, preferably metal, to get a nice straight edge. You will also need a square to make sure you are achieving perfect right angles. In order to mark perfect circles for the archways and portholes, a drafting compass will be needed.

Before doing any measuring and marking (which always leads to cutting), study the plans thoroughly, read through all the steps, and make sure you understand everything that is happening. Remember, as any carpenter will tell you, measure twice and cut once! I will say it again: measure twice and cut once.

The ark plans included in this book are at half scale (with the exception of the deck locks), so ½" (13mm) on paper is actually 1" (25mm) in reality. The plans are all marked on graph paper so that you can make sense of each measurement. I would strongly advise against photocopying all the plans at twice the scale; it is much more accurate to use the plans as a guide to manually mark out each component on your wood stock. One exception: Because the bowsprit has several curved lines to it, this one would be acceptable to use as a pattern (photocopy at 200%).

Please note that due to space limitations, the plans for the Hull Panel, Hull Bottom Panel, and Deck Panel show only half the length; simply mirror the other half to get the full component size.

CUTTING. I used my band saw for most of the woodcutting for this project. I relied on the off-the-shelf straight edges for some of the components, but plenty of other straight edges need to be cut manually. I have a comfort level and steady enough hand to freehand a straight cut on the band saw. If you do not feel comfortable with this method, use a gate on your band saw, or even use a table saw if you have access to one. Remember, we are not creating fine furniture here; this is a folk art project and a certain amount of roughness is acceptable. That said, you still need to be accurate on your measurements; otherwise, nothing will fit that way it should.

A scroll saw is needed to cut the portholes out of the cabin panels; you will need to drill a small hole within the marked circles so that you can fish the scroll saw blade through.

The ramp is removable and can be stored with the ark.

Always practice safety by wearing gloves, goggles, and hearing protection. Remember to take your time, don't force the cutting edge, and keep your hands away from the path of the blade.

Before cutting, make sure that you are cutting the correct line and that you are on the waste side of the line. Again, measure twice and cut once! Be sure to lightly sand all the sawed edges with 80-grit sandpaper.

GLUING AND CLAMPING. You will need at least two bar-style clamps, depending on how much you want to accomplish at one time, and at least two spring-style hand clamps. I use common yellow wood glue for joining all of the panels, with the help of brads or screws in some areas.

Before gluing and clamping, always perform a dry fit. Do this step on a flat, level surface, such as a bench top. Make sure that all components fit snugly and squarely; if not, now is the time to make an adjustment or scrap it and create a new piece.

Apply the glue as you wish, such as with a cotton swab or even your finger. Spread a thin layer along the edge of your panels. When clamping, excess glue will squeeze out; it is very important to clean off the excess immediately with a damp rag. If you don't do this now, the glue will very rudely show up when you begin the painting and finishing process.

Also, try to be generally neat when working with the glue. Keep your hands perpetually clean of it, or before you know it, you will have glue fingerprints all over your work.

When applying the shingles, a hot glue gun is a necessity. Why? If you try to use regular wood glue, you won't have an instant bond and the shingles will be sliding out of place—a very frustrating and quite ineffective way to work. Be sure to use construction-grade yellow, hot temperature glue sticks as opposed to the more common white craft glue. I cannot stress this enough: the white craft glue is not made to last, and it doesn't get hot enough to make a permanent bond. You will have shingles popping off later on, trust me. All it takes is one ¼" (6mm)-round bead of glue on the back of each shingle. Press the shingle into place firmly, and hold it there for about 5 or 6 seconds—instant bond!

Be very careful when handling the gun, and be sure to wear gloves when pressing the shingles into place; this glue is very hot and will most definitely burn you if it comes in contact with your skin. Keep a bowl of cool water handy. If you happen to get some glue on your skin, immediately dunk your hand into the water. The glue will instantly cool off and harden. You can then peel it off.

Remember to apply the hot glue sparingly. If you notice that some has squeezed out the side of the piece you are applying, simply let it harden then trim away the excess with a carving knife or a small X-Acto blade. Do not attempt to wipe it away—you will promptly burn yourself!

FASTENING. Some joints will be fine just to glue and clamp; other areas will need additional fastening, as you will see in the step-by-step demonstrations. I prefer to use an air-powered (pneumatic) brad gun for this task for several reasons: it is nice and quick, the brad holds much more effectively than a conventional nail, and it won't jar the project like hammering a nail into place would. Using a brad gun is, of course, an option; you may prefer to use a hammer and nails or may not have access to a brad gun. If you will be hammering by hand, I suggest using 1¼" (32mm) ribbed paneling nails; they have small heads like finishing nails, and the ribs prevent the components from pulling apart. Also, you will need a center punch to countersink the nail heads below the surface.

During steps 78 to 82, you will be attaching the completed cabin assembly to the surface of the deck panel. This step is accomplished by carefully gluing the cabin assembly in place, letting it dry, then driving screws into it from the bottom using predrilled holes as a guide. Why do I recommend this way? Imagine attempting to glue and drill all at once; there is no good way to position the cabin upside down while simultaneously holding the

deck panel and the drill, and all the while trying to line things up and drive the screw. Meanwhile, glue would be getting all over the deck panel surface. By letting the two components bond by glue first, you now have stability when driving the screws; the glue bond will be strong enough to hold things in position, but not permanently—that's what the screws are for.

RAMP. The ramp is a simple structure cut from a single piece of ¼" (6mm)-thick poplar stock, measuring 8" (203mm) by 5½" (140mm). A 5½" (140mm) length of ½" (13mm) square dowel rod is glued across the width of the underside, positioned ¾" (19mm) back from one edge. This piece of wood is meant as a "stop" when the ramp is placed in position over the threshold of the side opening of the ark. The ramp is finished in the same manner as the deck, with the same colors.

WEATHERVANE. I designed the weathervane to resemble the shape of a dove in descending flight. It is cut on the scroll saw from ¼" (6mm)-thick poplar wood stock, measuring 2½" (64mm) by 2¾" (70mm). I painted it using Neutral Grey (Americana) for the background and Antique White (Delta Ceramcoat) for the details, finishing and antiquing it in the same manner as the carvings. A small ³⁄₁₆" (5mm) hole was

Coat hanger wire helps birds perch on the peak of the ark.

drilled into the underside edge to accommodate a 3" (76mm) length of coat hanger wire, which serves as a pole. Once finished, it is to be inserted into the provided hole on top of the cupola. Using cyanoacrylate glue, adhere the pole into the weathervane itself, but do not glue it into the cupola; you will want to be able to remove it for storage.

FINAL NOTE. Remember that the instructions for this project are all merely guidelines; you can build your ark just as I have shown, or you can use my instructions as a bare-bones assembly in order to elaborate on the existing design. Depending on your experience and skill level, you can take this project considerably further than what is shown here.

Take your time, read all instructions carefully, be careful, and have a blast!

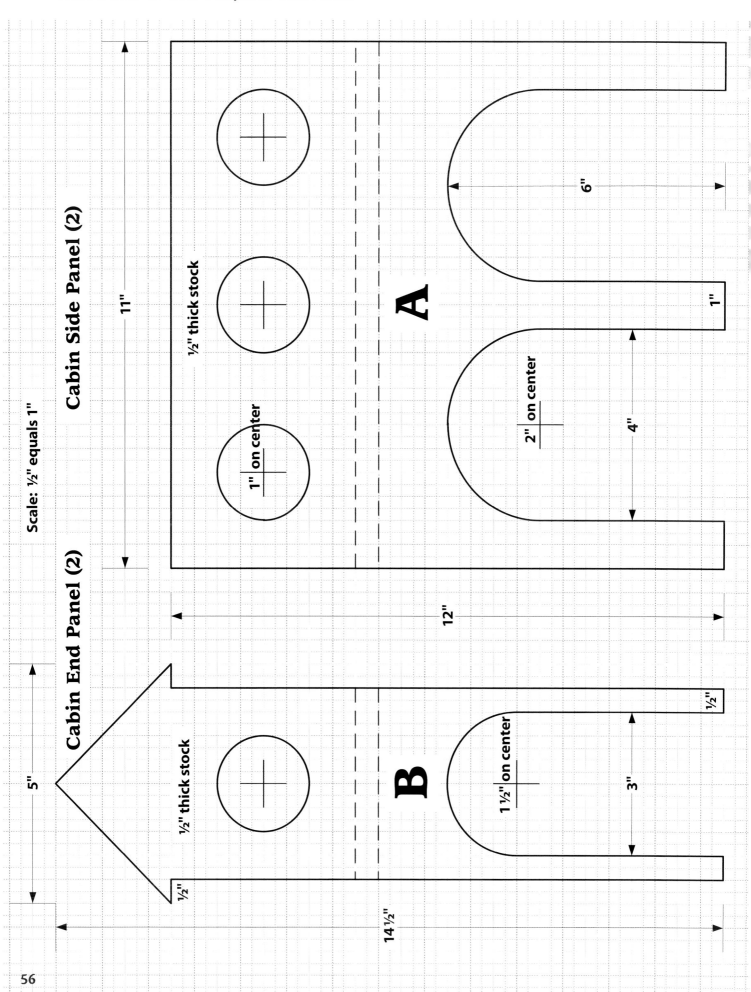

Scale: ½" equals 1"

Cabin Side Panel (2)

Cabin End Panel (2)

½" thick stock

A

11"

1"

6"

1" on center

2" on center

4"

12"

½" thick stock

B

½"

1½" on center

3"

½"

5"

14½"

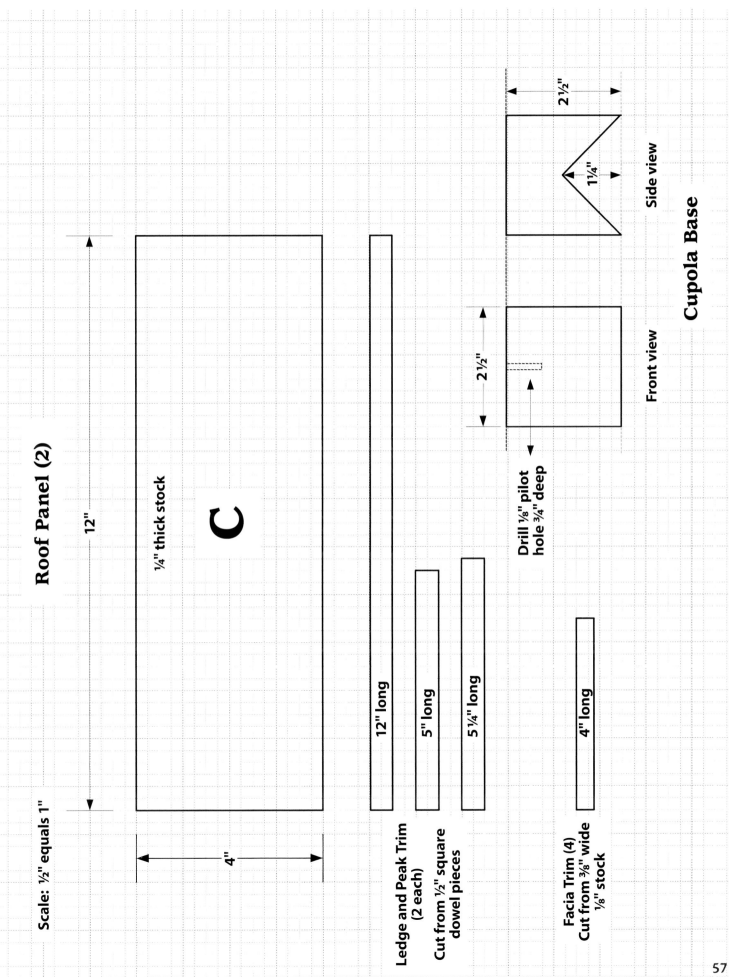

Roof Panel (2)

Scale: ½" equals 1"

12"

¼" thick stock

C

4"

12" long

5" long

5¼" long

4" long

Ledge and Peak Trim (2 each)
Cut from ½" square dowel pieces

Facia Trim (4)
Cut from ⅜" wide ⅛" stock

2½"

1¼"

Side view

2½"

Front view

Drill ⅛" pilot hole ¾" deep

Cupola Base

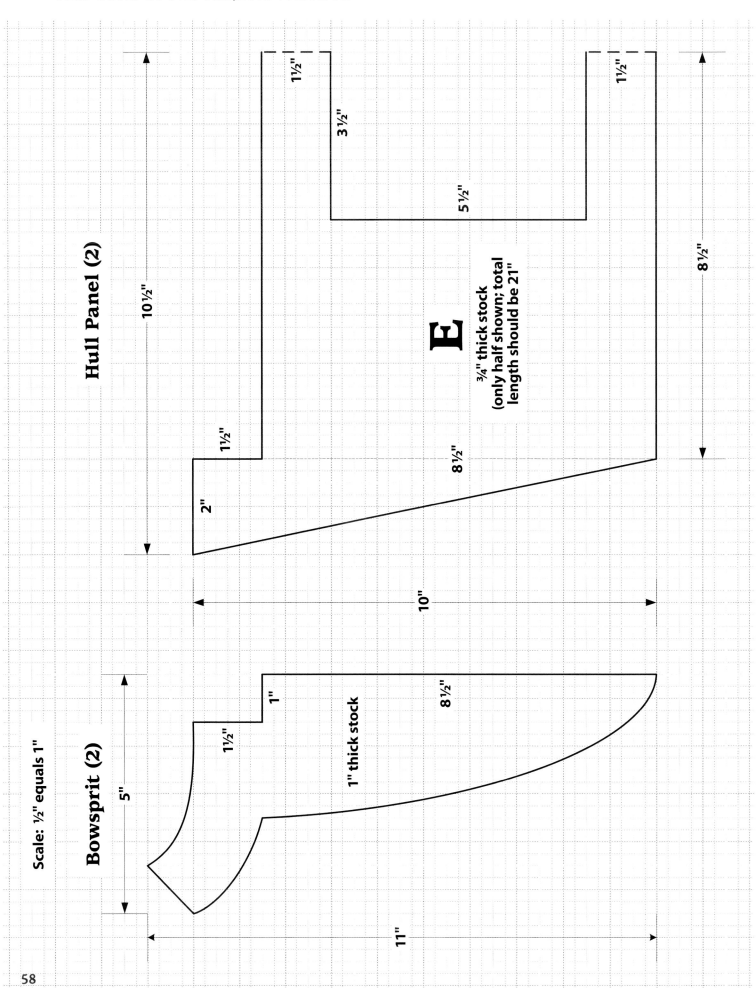

Hull Panel (2)

1½"

3½"

5½"

8½"

10½"

E

¾" thick stock
(only half shown; total
length should be 21"

1½"

2"

8½"

10"

Scale: ½" equals 1"

Bowsprit (2)

1"

1½"

8½"

1" thick stock

5"

11"

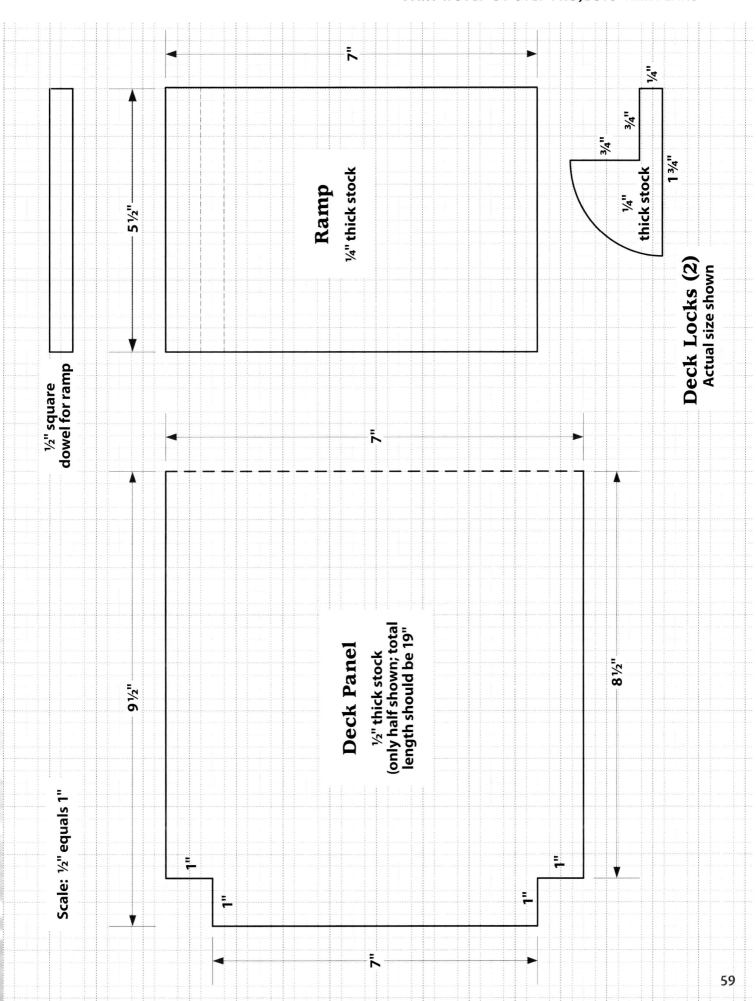

Scale: ½" equals 1"

½" square dowel for ramp

Ramp
¼" thick stock

5½"

7"

Deck Locks (2)
Actual size shown

¾"

¾"

¼"

¼"

1¾"

¼"
thick stock

Deck Panel
½" thick stock
(only half shown; total length should be 19")

9½"

7"

8½"

1"

1"

1"

1"

7"

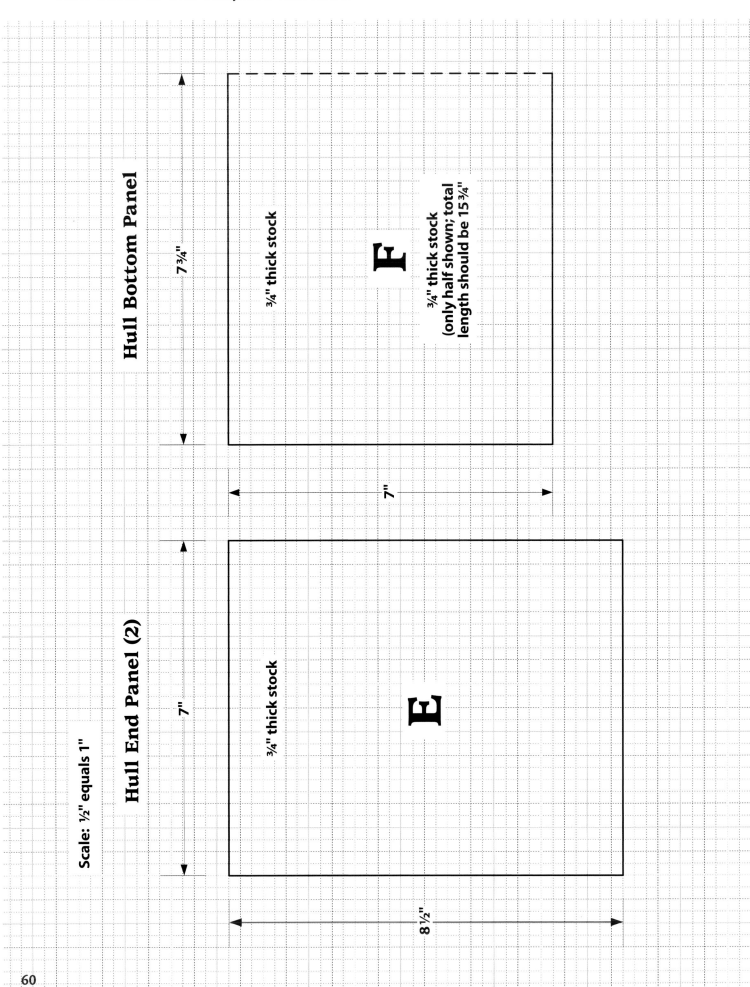

Hull Bottom Panel

7 ¾"

¾" thick stock

F

¾" thick stock
(only half shown; total
length should be 15 ¾"

7"

Scale: ½" equals 1"

Hull End Panel (2)

7"

¾" thick stock

E

8 ½"

Front

Back

Side

Removable Deck Lock

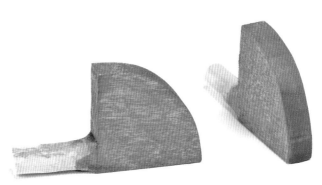

These tabs allow the deck to be removed for access to the storage area below.

Weathervane Pattern

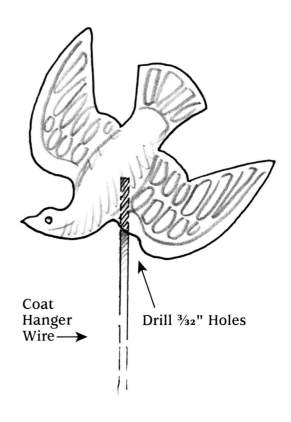

Coat Hanger Wire →

Drill ³⁄₃₂" Holes

PHOTOCOPY AT 100%

Top Half of the Ark

Bottom Half of the Ark

Materials: Construction

> Three 48" x 5½" (1219mm x 140mm) pieces of ½" (13mm)-thick poplar stock (Also called 4 x 6)

> One 3' x 6" (914mm x 152mm) piece of ¼" (6mm)-thick poplar stock

> One 24" x 48" (610mm x 1219mm) panel of prepackaged, laminated pine project board

> Two 11" x 5" (279mm x 127mm) pieces of 1" (25mm)-thick basswood stock

> One 2½" x 2½" x 2½" (64mm x 64mm x 64mm) basswood cube

> One store-bought, lathe-turned decorative wooden finial

> 50" (1270mm) of ½" (13mm) square poplar dowel rod

> 16" (406mm) of ⅛" (3mm)-thick ⅜" (10mm)-wide craft trim

> Large quantity of dollhouse shingles (optional)

> 51" (1295mm) length of miniature craft dental molding (optional)

> Yellow wood glue

> High temp construction-grade glue sticks to be used with hot glue gun

> Four 1" (25mm) general purpose wood screws

> ¼" (6mm) brads to be used with a nail gun OR a package of 1¼" (32mm) ribbed finishing nails (for wall paneling)

> Water-based wood putty for covering nail holes

Tools: Construction

> Straightedge, yardstick, or ruler

> Squaring tool

> Drafting compass

> 14" (356mm) band saw

> Scroll saw

> At least two bar clamps, 15" (381mm) or longer

> At least two spring style hand clamps

> Brad gun (air-powered) or hammer

> Power hand drill with ⅛" (3mm) and ¼" (6mm) drill bits

> High-temp hot glue gun

> Phillips screwdriver

> Cabinet scraper (optional)

> Center punch, if using nails

> ½" (13mm) fishtail gouge

> ⅜" (10mm) V-tool

> 80-grit sandpaper

> Cotton swabs for glue application (optional)

> Marking pencil

> Wet rag for cleaning glue

BUILDING THE ARK

1. **GLUE ADJOINING EDGES.** Apply yellow wood glue to the adjoining edges of two ½" x 5½" x 48" (13mm x 140mm x 1219mm) slats of poplar wood stock. Carefully and evenly clamp them together on edge, using three bar-style clamps. Let the boards dry overnight on a flat, even surface.

2. **SCRAPE THE GLUE JOINT.** Using a steel hand scraper, scrape the glue joint to a smooth finish on both sides. You could sand the joint smooth, but the scraper is quicker and more efficient.

3. **MARK THE ARCHES.** Measure 12" (305mm) in from the end of your 11" x 48" (279mm x 1219mm) laminated board, and cut, using a saw of your choice. You now have an 11" x 12" (279mm x 305mm) piece, which will serve as Side Panel A of the ark's cabin. Referring to the plans, measure and mark out the two archway openings with a compass.

4. **CUT THE ARCHES.** Using a band saw, carefully cut the archway openings.

5. **MARK THE PORTHOLES.** Referring to the plans, measure and mark the porthole openings. Use a compass for this step.

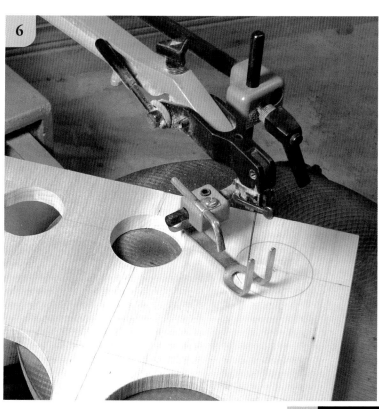

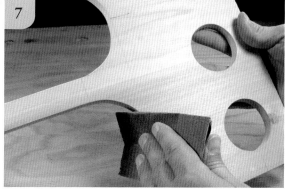

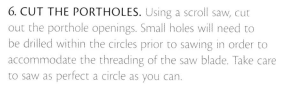

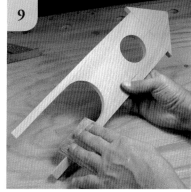

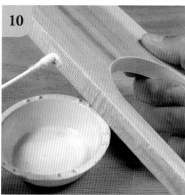

6. CUT THE PORTHOLES. Using a scroll saw, cut out the porthole openings. Small holes will need to be drilled within the circles prior to sawing in order to accommodate the threading of the saw blade. Take care to saw as perfect a circle as you can.

7. SAND THE CUT EDGES. Using 80-grit sandpaper, lightly hand sand all cut edges and outer corners so they are smooth to the touch. Repeat steps 3 to 7 to create 2 identical cabin side panels. You will have 24" (610mm) of the laminate board for later use.

8. MEASURE END PANEL B. Using a fresh slat of ½" x 5½" x 48" (13mm x 140mm x 1219mm) poplar stock, cut a length measuring 5" (127mm) wide and 14½" (368mm) long. Referring to the plans, mark and measure all specifics for End Panel B, as shown.

9. CUT END PANEL B. Cut out End Panel B in the same manner as previously instructed. Lightly sand the edges. Repeat steps 9 and 10 to make 2 identical cabin end panels (B).

10. APPLY WOOD GLUE. Use a cotton swab to apply yellow wood glue to both edges of 1 End Panel B (do not apply glue to the peaked angles on top).

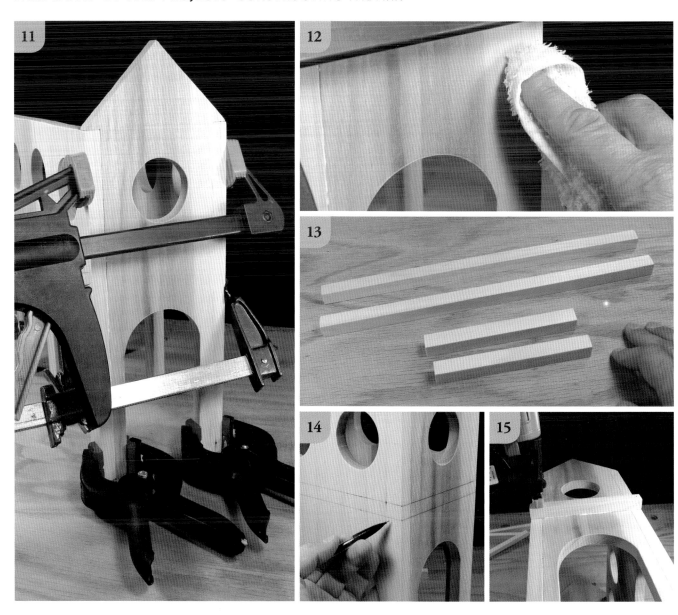

11. CLAMP THE PANELS. Assemble both A panels with the glued-up B panel, fitting them flush with the precut insets. Once the 3 panels are in place, clamp them tightly together with the bar clamps. Make sure the surface is flush before tightening the clamps. Smaller hand clamps hold the bottom sections in place.

12. ADD THE FINAL END PANEL. Once the clamps are in place and tightened, use a wet rag to quickly wipe away any excess glue that may have squeezed out of the joints. Excess dried glue on the surface will affect your painting later on. Let the piece dry overnight on a flat, even surface. Glue and assemble the remaining End Panel B on the other side. Note: If you have enough clamps, you can glue all 4 panels at once.

13. CUT THE DOWEL. Using ½" (13mm) square poplar dowel rod, cut two 12" (305mm) lengths and two 5" (127mm) lengths. Sand the ends smooth.

14. MARK THE DOWEL PLACEMENT. Referring to the plans, measure and mark where the square dowel pieces will be attached, 7½" (191mm) up from the bottom.

15. SECURE THE SHORT DOWEL PIECES. Apply glue to one of the 5" (127mm) dowel pieces, and put it in place on 1 End panel B. Make sure it is centered and flush with each edge. While holding it in place secure it with a brad gun—1 brad on each side, straight into the corner of both panels. Attach the remaining 5" (127mm) dowel piece to the opposite side in the same manner.

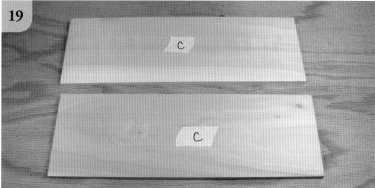

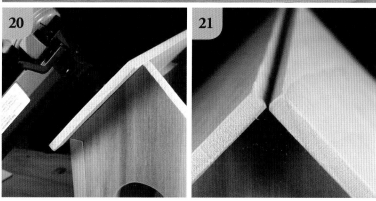

16. SECURE THE LONG DOWEL PIECES. Attach the 12" (305mm) pieces in the same manner, aligning them with the 5" (127mm) pieces. One brad into each end is sufficient—just enough to hold the pieces securely while the glue dries. The result is an even ledge the whole way around.

17. PAINT THE INSIDE OF THE CABIN. Paint the inside of the cabin now, before the roof is attached. Use a ½" (13mm) flat brush, and apply 2 coats of full strength Rookwood Red.

18. PROGRESS SO FAR. If you have been careful with your measurements, cuts, and laminating, the cabin will be solid and square.

19. CUT THE ROOF PANELS. Referring to the plans, measure, cut, and sand two 12" x 4" (305mm x 10mm) C panels from ¼" (6mm) poplar stock. These will form the roof.

20. ASSEMBLE THE C PANELS. Apply glue to the angled peak edges on the cabin, then place 1 C panel in position, evenly distributing the ½" (13mm) hangover on each side. Make sure the top edge of the roof panel is flush with the peak, as shown. Affix it in place with the brad gun, 1 brad on each side. Attach the other C panel in the same manner.

21. RESULT. Both C panels are in place. Notice the closeup of the peak; correct installation of both panels should leave a V-shaped gap in the top, as shown.

22. BAND SAW THE CUPOLA BASE. Referring to the plans, band saw the cupola base. I used basswood, because it will be carved.

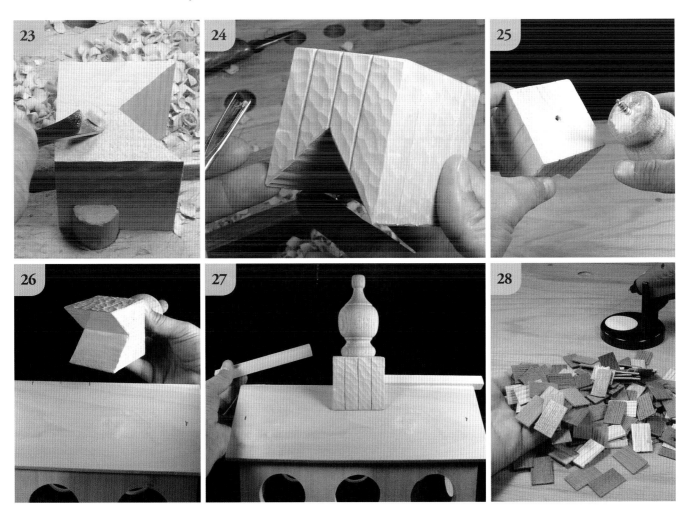

23. CARVE THE SURFACE. Using a ½" (13mm) fishtail gouge, tool the surface of the cupola base. Skim just enough off to erase the saw marks. Work all sides and the top.

24. ADD GROOVES. Using a ⅜" (10mm) V-tool, carve evenly spaced vertical grooves into each side of the cupola base. The lines give the base the effect of wainscoting.

25. ADD THE FINIAL. Find the center on the top, and drill a ⅛" (3mm) guide hole. Apply glue to the base of a store-bought decorative wooden finial. Simply screw it into the hole until it is tight. Wipe away any excess glue.

26. ATTACH THE CUPOLA TO THE ROOF. Find and mark the center of the roof. Generously glue up the bottom angle-cut portion of the cupola base, and firmly press it into place, dead center. Measure both sides to make sure it is evenly spaced.

27. ADD DOWEL PIECES. Cut two ½" (13mm) square dowel pieces to 5¼" (133mm) each. Glue them into position, fitting them snugly into the V-shaped gap at the roof's peak and pushing them tightly up against the cupola base. They should each hang over the edge ½" (13mm).

28. PREPARE THE SHINGLES. I buy premade cedar shingles for dollhouses. You may also make your own from scrap wood. Use a hot glue gun; the glue dries fast, and the shingles don't slide out of place. Be sure to use high-temp wood glue sticks, not the white low-temp ones.

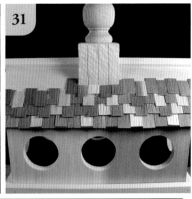

29. APPLY THE FIRST ROW OF SHINGLES. Start with the lowest course. Be sure to hang them over a bit, and place them randomly at slightly uneven heights in respect to each other; this arrangement will add to the folksy effect. If your shingles vary in color as mine do, be sure to apply them randomly.

30. ADD THE SECOND ROW. When laying the second course, overlap the first course and offset the shingles. You will need to cut the last one in half to meet the edge of the roof. Proceed in this manner all the way up.

31. FIT THE SHINGLES AROUND THE CUPOLA. When you reach the cupola, cut the shingles to fit around it. Dry fit the pieces, then glue them in place. Your work doesn't have to be perfect; remember this is folk art and rustic charm is the objective. Glue the shingles securely.

32. APPLY THE LAST ROW. Finish up the last course, cutting each shingle as short as you need to in order to complete the appearance. Be sure to glue them snugly against the square dowel at the peak.

33. THE FINISHED EFFECT. Be sure to trim any shingles that hang over the sides with a knife so they are flush with the edge. Repeat steps 29 to 33 to complete the other side.

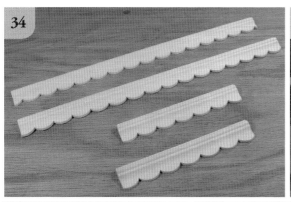

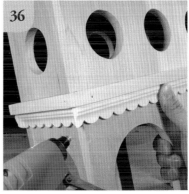

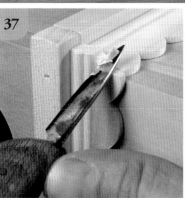

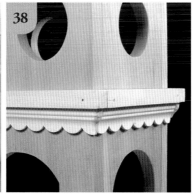

34. CUT THE DENTAL MOLDING. Precut 4 pieces of store-bought decorative dental molding. You'll need 2 at 5" (127mm) long and 2 at 11½" (292mm) long.

35. ATTACH THE SHORT MOLDING PIECES. Using the hot glue gun, attach one 5" (127mm) molding piece underneath the dowel ledge. Carefully align it so the ends are flush with the corners of the cabin. Hold the molding in place a few seconds until it is secure. Attach the other 5" (127mm) piece in the same manner.

36. ATTACH THE LONG MOLDING PIECES. Now glue the 11½" (292mm) pieces on each remaining side. Make sure the corners are tightly bound. Allow any excess glue to dry, then trim it away with your carving knife.

37. CARVE THE CORNERS. Once all of the trim pieces are secure, carve the corners to shape with a carving knife, as shown. Try to follow the contour of the end pieces, and make sure each corner is smooth to the touch.

38. THE FINISHED RESULT. Double check that all the shingles and pieces of molding are secure before moving on to the next step of the ark assembly.

39. ADD THE FASCIA PIECES. Referring to the plans, precut 4 fascia pieces from ⅛" (3mm)-thick, ⅜" (10mm)-wide store-bought craft stock. Sand the ends, and hot glue each piece to the edges of the ¼" (6mm) roof panels, as shown. Be sure that the bottom edge of the fascia is flush with the inside edge of the roof panels.

40. THE FINISHED EFFECT. Notice that the fascia trim caps off the end nicely and also protects the exposed edges of the shingles.

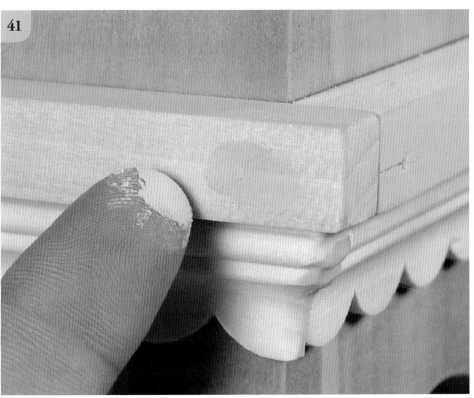

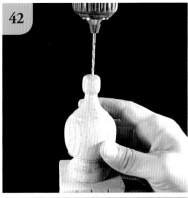

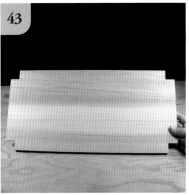

41. COVER THE BRAD HOLES. Using a water-based wood filler and your finger, fill in all the brad holes. Once the wood filler is dry, lightly sand it smooth.

42. DRILL A HOLE FOR THE WEATHERVANE. Drill a ⅛" (3mm) hole in the top of the cupola so a weathervane can be installed later.

43. CUT THE DECK. Referring to the plans, measure, mark, cut, and sand the remaining 11½" x 24" (292mm x 610mm) laminated poplar board (from step 1) to fashion the ark's deck. The finished piece measures 9" x 19" (229mm x 483mm) and has 1" (25mm) notches in each corner. Set it aside for now.

44. MEASURE THE HULL. Referring to the plans, mark and measure the Hull Panel D, as shown, from store-bought ¾" (19mm)-thick laminated pine project board.

45. CUT THE HULL. Using the band saw, cut the hull panel to shape.

46. CUT THE HATCH OPENING. Using a scroll saw, cut the side hatch opening in the hull panel.

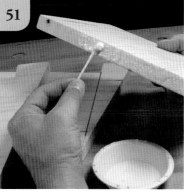

47. SAND THE HULL. After the hull panel is cut to shape, lightly sand all edges and corners with 80-grit sandpaper so they are smooth to the touch.

48. CUT A SECOND PANEL. Cut a second identical D panel, minus the hatch opening. Both panels are shown in completion.

49. CUT THE ADDITIONAL HULL PANELS. Referring to the plans, measure, mark, cut, and sand 2 E Hull End Panels and 1 F Hull Bottom Panel. Use the ¾" (19mm)-thick laminated pine stock here as well.

50. MARK THE INNER SIDES. Determine which side is the least attractive on each D panel; these will be the inner sides. The vertical guide mark should line up with the inside upper notch and the bottom corner; the horizontal line should be 1½" (38mm) up from the bottom. Both lines should form a 90-degree angle. Mark both ends on the inner side of each D panel in this manner.

51. APPLY GLUE. Apply yellow wood glue to both 8½" (216mm) edges of one E panel.

52. ASSEMBLE THE PANELS. Assemble both D hull panels and the E panel by aligning the outer surface of the E panel with the drawn guide marks, as shown.

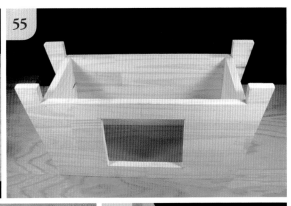

53. CLAMP THE PANELS. Use bar clamps, making sure that the E panel is in perfect alignment with the guide mark before tightening the clamps. Also be sure that the bottom of the E panel is flat against the bench surface.

54. SECURE THE PANELS WITH BRADS. Once clamped and in place, further secure the panels with the brad gun, nailing into the side of the D panel and the edge of the E panel. One brad near the top, one near the bottom, and one in the center will be sufficient. Nail both sides. Allow the glue to dry overnight.

55. ASSEMBLE THE OTHER END. Repeat steps 51 to 54 to assemble the other end. The top edges should be flush and level with each other (with the exception of the raised corner projections).

56. INSERT THE BOTTOM PANEL. Insert the F Hull Bottom Panel from the bottom, as shown. It should be a fairly tight fit, so glue is not required; it would make quite a mess anyway.

57. TAP THE PANEL INTO POSITION. Using a carving mallet or a hammer, lightly tap the bottom panel into position. Align the top surface of the panel with the horizontal guide marks (the ark is shown here upside down).

58. SECURE THE PANEL WITH BRADS. Notice that the top surface of the F panel is flush and level with the bottom edge of the hatch opening. Once the panel is in place, secure it with 3 brads on each side.

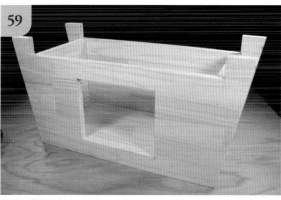

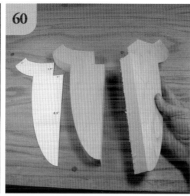

59. THE ASSEMBLED HULL. The bottom panel is in place, and the basic hull structure is fully assembled.

60. CUT THE BOWSPRITS. Referring to the plans, measure, mark, and cut the bowsprits. I used 1" (25mm)-thick basswood stock, because we will be carving it.

61. CARVE THE SURFACE. While held in place with a vise, start tooling the surface with the ½" (13mm) fishtail, just enough to erase the saw marks.

62. TEXTURE THE SURFACE. Texture the outer edges and the other side as well.

63. CARVE THE GROOVES. Using the ⅜" (10mm) V-tool, carve grooves that represent planks, as if the bowsprit were constructed of boards. Complete both bowsprits in this manner.

64. MARK THE BOWSPRITS' POSITIONS. Find and mark the center of one end of the assembled hull. Draw a 1" (25mm)-wide guideline strip where the bowsprit will be attached. Draw guidelines on the other side as well.

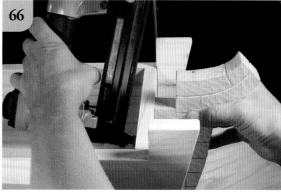

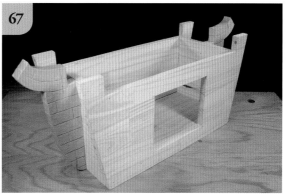

65. APPLY GLUE. Apply glue to the inner straight edge of the bowsprit, as shown.

66. ATTACH THE FIRST BOWSPRIT. While holding the bowsprit firmly and accurately in place, use the brad gun to attach it from the inside of the hull. Three evenly spaced brads should do it.

67. ATTACH THE SECOND BOWSPRIT. Repeat steps 65 and 66 to attach the remaining bowsprit to the opposite side.

68. CUT THE MOLDING. Cut and sand 2 lengths of the decorative dental molding, each 17" (432mm) long.

69. GLUE THE MOLDING IN PLACE. Apply hot glue evenly across the back of 1 piece, and firmly press it into place, flush with the top edge of the hull. The molding should fit perfectly between both raised corner projections. Complete the other side as well.

70. THE HULL IS COMPLETELY ASSEMBLED. Paint the inside with 2 coats of full-strength Graphite, using a 1" (25mm) general purpose finishing brush.

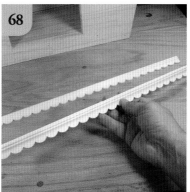

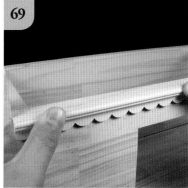

BUILDING THE ARK

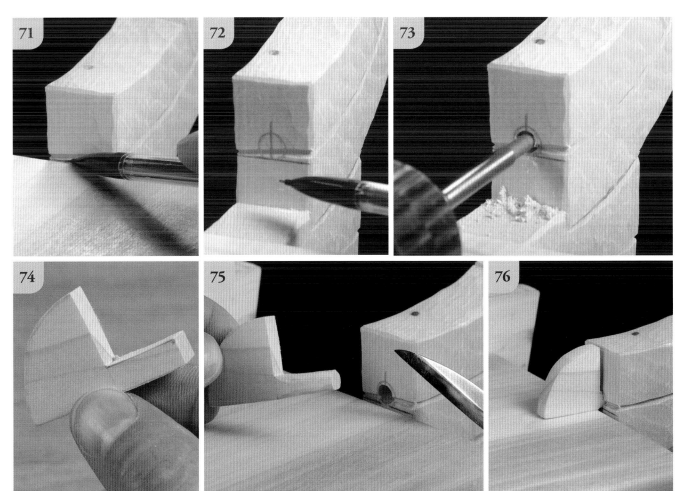

71. PUT THE DECK IN PLACE. Take the ark's deck (prepared in step 43), and lay it in place over the hull. It should fit like a glove. Do not permanently attach the deck; you will want to take the ark apart for storing purposes. With the deck in place, mark the inside of the bowsprit, indicating the where the deck's surface is, as shown. Mark both ends.

72. MARK HOLES FOR THE BOWSPRIT. Remove the deck. Based on where the marks are, make another mark indicating where a ¼" (6mm) hole will be drilled into the bowsprit. The hole should be just above the surface of the deck. Mark the other end in the same manner.

73. DRILL HOLES FOR THE BOWSPRIT. Using a hand drill with a ¼" (6mm) drill bit, drill a hole straight in, about ¾" (19mm) deep, as level as possible. Drill a hole in the other end as well.

74. CUT THE DECK LOCKS. Referring to the plans, prepare a deck lock, as shown (you will need 2). Cut them from ¼" (6mm)-thick poplar stock with the scroll saw. Make sure the wood grain runs along the length of the skinny ¼" (6mm) extension for strength.

75. SHAPE THE DECK LOCK. Using the carving knife, whittle the ¼" (6mm) extended portion of the deck lock into a rounded dowel shape. Do a little at a time, constantly trying to fit the extension into the drilled hole, so that it eventually fits snugly all the way in.

76. FIT THE DECK LOCK IN PLACE. The deck locks keep the deck securely in place when the ark is on display. They can be removed when you wish to disassemble the ark. Fit the other deck lock in place.

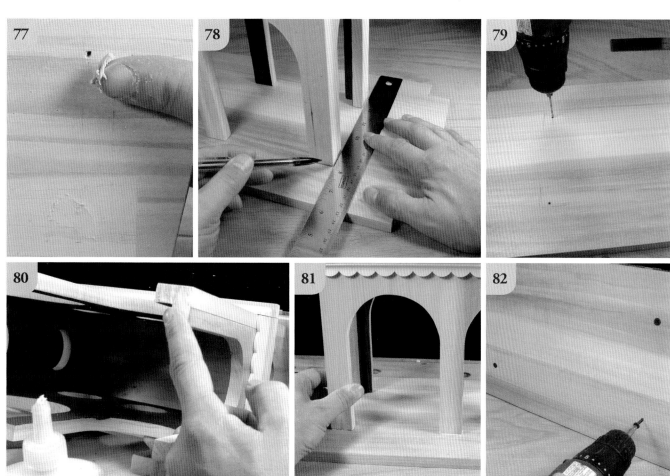

77. COVER THE BRAD HOLES. Using a water-based wood filler and your finger, fill in all the brad holes. Once the wood filler is dry, lightly sand it smooth.

78. MARK THE PLACEMENT OF THE CABIN. Remove the deck. Using a ruler or yardstick, center the cabin assembly on the deck surface. There should be an equal distance of 2" (51mm) on each side and an equal distance of 4" (102mm) on each end. Mark each of the cabin's outer corner legs on the deck's surface.

79. DRILL HOLES FOR THE CABIN ASSEMBLY. Remove the cabin assembly. Using the marks as a guide, drill one ⅛" (3mm) hole at each corner. Position them so that they are about ¼" (6mm) inside the mark, as shown.

80. APPLY GLUE. Apply glue to the underside of all 6 legs of the cabin assembly.

81. GLUE THE CABIN IN PLACE. With the deck lying on a table top, carefully place the cabin assembly in position on the deck surface. Press down. Immediately clean up any excess glue with a wet rag. Once the cabin assembly is in place, do not disturb it, letting it dry in position overnight.

82. ADD SCREWS. Once dry, turn the cabin and deck assembly on its side. Now that the glue has secured the cabin in place, further strengthen the bond by driving 1" (25mm) screws through the ⅛" (3mm) drilled holes from the bottom up.

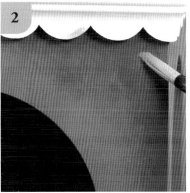

Tools and Materials: Painting

> ½" (13mm) flat brush
> Old ¼" (6mm) round brush for stippling effect
> 1" (25mm) general purpose staining brush
> Clean cotton rag
> Fast-drying satin polyurethane
> Brown gel wood stain

Paint Colors

> Country Red / Americana
> Rookwood Red / Americana
> Celery Green / Americana
> Light Avocado / Americana
> School Bus Yellow / Americana
> Raw Sienna / FolkArt
> Antique Gold / Americana
> Graphite / Americana

1. PAINT THE LOWER PORTION OF THE CABIN. Using a ½" (13mm) flat brush, begin to apply Country Red to the lower portion of the cabin. Keep a wet edge on the brush to keep the paint slightly thinned with water; you want to see a bit of the wood showing through here. Be sure to paint the inner edges of the arched openings as well.

2. STIPPLE ADDITIONAL COLOR. Using a ¼" (6mm) round brush, apply Rookwood Red in a stippling effect. Apply the paint sparingly in layers; the color should be heavier toward the outer corners and blend to light as you move inward.

3. THE LOWER CABIN IS COMPLETE. Notice how the stippling is heavier at the base of the feet and between the arches. The whole effect provides an antique look.

4. PAINT THE UPPER PORTION OF THE CABIN. Using the ½" (13mm) flat brush, begin to apply Celery Green to the upper portion of the cabin. Remember to keep the paint slightly thinned with water. Be sure to paint the inner edges of the porthole openings as well.

5. STIPPLE ADDITIONAL COLOR. Using the ¼" (6mm) round stippling brush, stipple around the portholes with Light Avocado, as shown.

6. THE UPPER CABIN IS COMPLETE. Note the effect of the stippling.

7. PAINT THE MOLDING. Using the ½" (13mm) flat brush, apply School Bus Yellow to the ledge and dental molding section. Because of the nature of the yellow pigment, you may have to give it a second coat.

8. PAINT THE FASCIA. Apply the yellow to the fascia, under the eaves, and to the square dowel in the peak.

9. PAINT THE CUPOLA. Apply the yellow to the cupola base as well.

10. PAINT THE FINIAL. Paint the finial as you wish. I alternated between the Country Red and Celery Green, as shown.

11. ADD WASHES OF COLOR TO THE LEDGE. Using the ¼" (6mm) round stippling brush, "dirty up" the bright yellow by applying varying washes of Raw Sienna to the outer corners of the ledge.

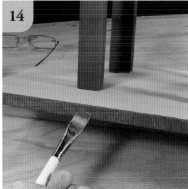

12. ADD WASHES TO REMAINING AREAS. Apply these Raw Sienna washes to all other yellow areas.

13. PAINT THE DECK. Using the ½" (13mm) flat brush, apply a thinned coat of Antique Gold to the deck surface.

14. PAINT THE DECK EDGES. Using the ½" (13mm) flat brush, apply Country Red to the deck's edges.

15. STIPPLE THE SURFACE. Using the ¼" (6mm) round stippling brush, stipple around the outer areas of the deck's surface with thinned Raw Sienna, as shown.

16. THE DECK IS COMPLETE. Make sure all areas are painted to your liking before moving on to paint the remainder of the ark.

17. APPLY A WASH TO THE HULL. Use a 1" (25mm) multipurpose staining brush to apply a very thinned wash of Raw Sienna to the body of the hull. This effect should be more of a stained look than a painted one to take advantage of the laminated pine's prominent grain pattern. Moisten the surface with plain water before applying the color.

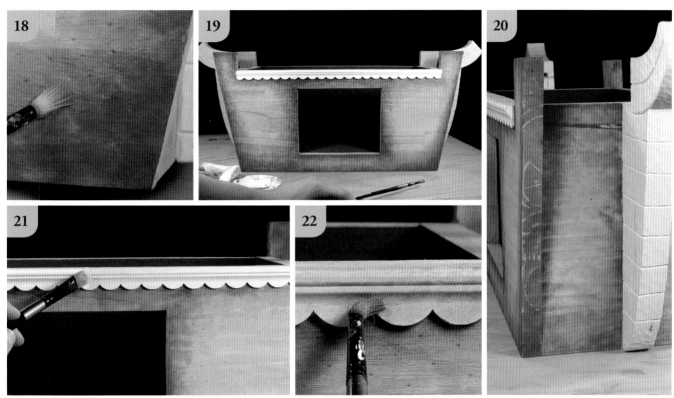

18. STIPPLE THE HULL. Using the ¼" (6mm) round stippling brush, stipple around the outer areas of the hull's surface with thinned Rookwood Red, as shown. Be sure to apply it in thin layers, making the color stronger toward the edges. Blending is very important here.

19. CONTINUE STIPPLING. Use the same technique over all areas of the laminated pine areas, as shown.

20. THE FINISHED EFFECT.

21. PAINT THE MOLDING. Using the ½" (13mm) flat brush, apply School Bus Yellow to the dental molding. Because of the nature of the yellow pigment, you may have to give it a second coat.

22. ADD A WASH. Using the ¼" (6mm) round stippling brush, "dirty up" the bright yellow by applying varying washes of Raw Sienna to the outer ends, as we did to the cabin's ledge.

23. PAINT THE BOWSPRITS. Using the 1" (25mm) multipurpose brush, apply a thinned coat of Celery Green to the bowsprits.

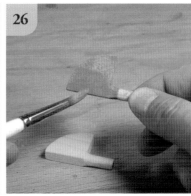

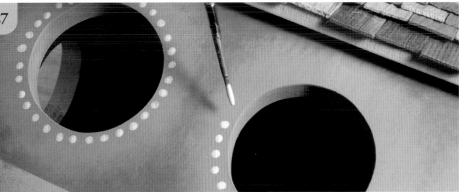

24. STIPPLE THE SURFACE. Using the ¼" (6mm) round stippling brush, stipple around the outer areas of the bowsprit's surface with thinned Light Avocado Green, as shown.

25. THE FINISHED EFFECT.

26. PAINT THE DECK LOCKS. Remember to paint the deck locks with a thinned coat of Light Avocado Green.

27. ADD A DECORATIVE FINISH. As a final optional detail (and to add to the ark's folk art theme), I added small dots of Antique White around the cabin's portholes with a ⅛" (3mm) round brush. Apply the dots consistently in size and spacing; otherwise, the painting will look messy.

28. CONTINUE AS NECESSARY. I added the dots around all the portholes and arches, and along the red edges of the deck.

29. APPLY SATIN POLYURETHANE. Make sure all paint has dried. Then, using the general purpose staining brush, apply a very thin coat of satin polyurethane to the entire cabin and deck assembly, inside and out. Be sure to scrub it into every nook and cranny, especially in the shingled areas.

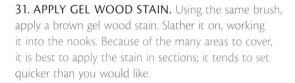

30. ALLOW THE ARK TO DRY. Do the same for the entire hull assembly, inside and out. Let the cabin and hull assemblies dry overnight.

31. APPLY GEL WOOD STAIN. Using the same brush, apply a brown gel wood stain. Slather it on, working it into the nooks. Because of the many areas to cover, it is best to apply the stain in sections; it tends to set quicker than you would like.

32. WIPE OFF EXCESS STAIN. Immediately wipe off the excess gel with a clean cotton rag. Continue to stain a section and wipe off the excess until the entire cabin and deck assembly are finished.

33. STAIN THE ROOF. When treating the shingled area, be sure to work the stain thoroughly into all the nooks. Be just as thorough when wiping away the excess.

34. STAIN UNDER THE EAVES. Remember to treat the hidden areas as well, such as those under the eaves. It is not necessary to antique the inside of the cabin or the hull.

35. ALLOW THE ARK TO DRY. Apply the antiquing technique to all surfaces of the hull assembly as well. Let both assemblies dry overnight before handling.

PAINTING THE ARK

PART II
PATTERNS

On the following pages you'll find patterns for Noah's wife and animals to populate your ark. I've included bears, sheep, elephants, and even a whale. All of the patterns are to be used at 100%. With some imagination and a few alterations, you can turn the more than 20 animals here into dozens to fill your ark.

BEARS

Basswood block: 6" x 3¼" x 2"
  (152mm x 83mm x 51mm)

Grain direction: Vertical
  or horizontal

The bear, a symbol of strength and raw primal power, has been worshipped in many ancient cultures both as benevolent and evil spirits. The bear is Finland's national animal and is well known as a political symbol for the country of Russia.

Being mostly found in the northern hemisphere, bears are overwhelmingly solitary creatures and are almost never spotted in groups, aside from a mother rearing her cubs. Although they are opportunistic meat eaters, the larger part of any bear's diet is vegetarian, except for polar bears, who eat mostly seals and fish.

During the Middle Ages, bears were thought to give birth to shapeless and eyeless lumps of flesh. The mother would then shape it to its proper form by licking it. This belief is where the expression "to lick something into shape" comes from.

Although the many species vary greatly in physical attributes, I chose to design this project based on a common brown bear, such as the grizzly or Kodiak. The design shows the bear in full stride, on all fours. Although the same pattern is to be used for both the male and female, I implemented a few changes in order to provide a little variety between the two: I "mirrored" the positions of the legs between the genders, used different shades of brown paint, and carved the female's head slightly less broad and her rear end a little more broad than the male (no offense, ladies).

Your beginning block before sawing will need to measure 6" (152mm) wide by 3¼" (83mm) high, with a thickness of 2" (51mm). Because this project is small, you will only need to saw the provided side pattern image. Although the grain direction should be vertical for most projects in this book, it is not absolutely necessary for this one because the bear's legs are quite stout.

Right Side

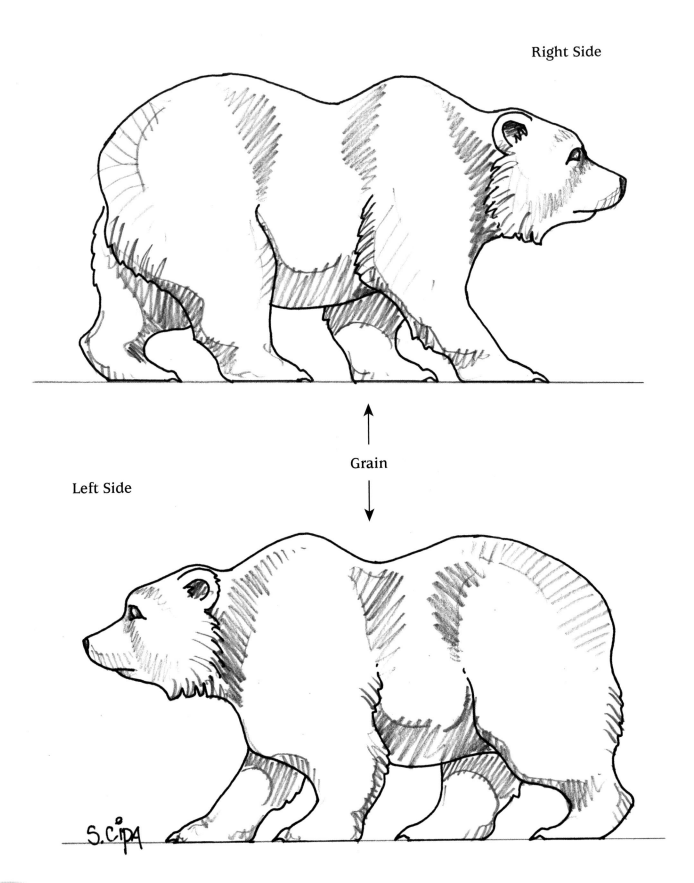

Grain

Left Side

S. CIPA

PHOTOCOPY AT 100%

Left Side

Front   Male

Back

Right Side

Top

Front

Left Side

Female

Back

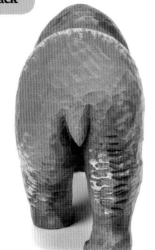

Right Side

Top

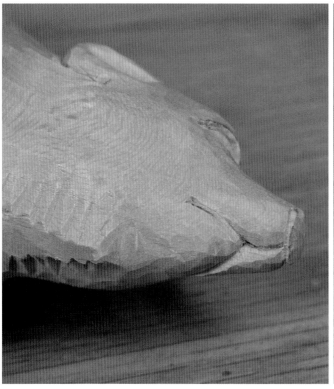

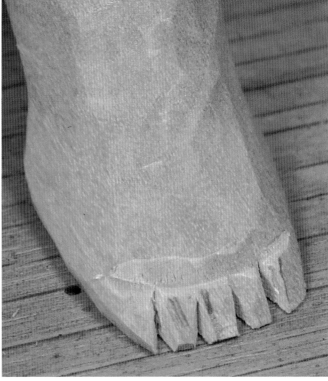

A view from the underside of the bear's head shows how the lower jaw meets the upper jaw.

Simple notches separate the bear's toes.

Face and front detail.

Paint Colors: Male

> Dark Chocolate / Americana
> (overall base color, irises)

> Country Twill / FolkArt
> (highlights, fur detail)

> Black / Americana (lowlights,
> eye base, nose, claws)

> Snow White / Americana
> (reflective light dot on pupil)

Paint Colors: Female

> Raw Sienna / FolkArt
> (overall base color)

> Burnt Umber / FolkArt (lowlights)

> Country Twill / FolkArt (fur detail)

> Black / Americana
> (eye base, nose, claws)

> Dark Chocolate / Americana (irises)

> Snow White / Americana
> (reflective light dot on pupil)

Tip
Watch for the subtle differences between the male and the female, including their leg positions and the shape of their hindquarters.

PART II: PATTERNS

PELICANS

Birds have long been associated with spirituality and the divine. This special status probably came about as the ancients first observed them in flight; birds became supernatural links to the heavens and earth.

The male and female pelicans use the same pattern; the only carved difference is that the male has spiky head feathers and the female has only one. They each have their own color palette as well.

Your beginning block before sawing will need to measure 2¼" (57mm) wide by 3" (76mm) high, with a thickness of 1¼" (32mm). The grain should be vertical.

Tip
Use care when carving the delicate head feathers.

Left Side

Right Side

Top

Front

Back

Basswood block: 2¼" x 3" x 1¼"
(57mm x 76mm x 32mm)
Grain direction: Vertical

Paint Colors: Male

> Black / Americana
(body, eye base, pupils)
> Neutral Grey / Americana
(lower layer of wings)
> Country Twill / FolkArt
(upper wing portion)
> Burnt Umber / FolkArt
(upper wing portion lowlights)
> Autumn Leaves / JoAnn Craft
Essentials (bill, feet)
> Snow White / Americana
(head, irises)

Paint Colors: Female

> Blue Stoneware / Apple
Barrel (body)
> Blue Haze / Americana
(lowlights on body)
> Black / Americana (eye base,
pupils, lowlights on bill and feet)
> Country Twill / FolkArt
(upper wing portion)
> Burnt Umber / FolkArt
(upper wing portion lowlights)
> Snow White / Americana
(head, lower layer of wings)
> Light Blue / FolkArt (lower layer
of wings lowlights, irises)
> Neutral Grey / Americana
(bill, feet)

S.CiPA

PHOTOCOPY AT 100%

FLAMINGOES

Why flamingoes? Why not? They're colorful and wacky enough to add some folk art flavor to this project.

Use the same pattern for both genders. Your beginning block before sawing will need to measure 2" (51mm) wide by 2½" (64mm) high, with a thickness of ¾" (19mm). The grain should be vertical. The legs are made from 2¾" (70mm)-long lengths of coat hanger wire. The base is cut from a bark-on natural stick of white birch about 1¾" (44mm) in diameter; however, you may use whatever you wish for the base. Drill ³⁄₁₆" (5mm) holes in both the flamingo's body and the base to accommodate the wire legs. Assemble all parts with cyanoacrylate glue. I painted a bit of blue water where the legs meet the base to suggest shallow water.

Tip
Create the legs from coat hanger wire.

Left Side

Right Side

Front

Back

Top

The coat hanger legs of the flamingo fit into holes drilled into the base.

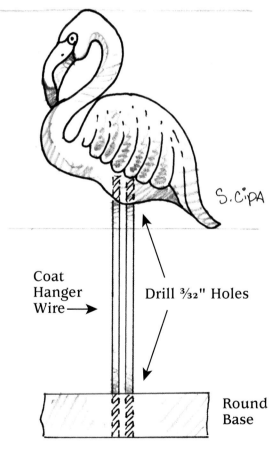

S. Cipa

Coat Hanger Wire →

Drill ³/₃₂" Holes

Round Base

PHOTOCOPY AT 100%

Basswood block: 2" x 2½" x ¾"
(51mm x 164mm x 19mm)
Grain direction: Vertical

Paint Colors

› Boysenberry Pink / Americana (entire body and legs)
› Black / Americana (tip of beak, pupils)
› Antique White / Delta Ceramcoat
 (face / beak, wing highlights)
› Light Blue / FolkArt (water on base)

TOUCANS

Why toucans? They're almost as wacky as flamingoes and just as colorful. Use the same pattern for both genders.

Your beginning block before sawing will need to measure 1½" (38mm) wide by 2" (51mm) high, with a thickness of ¾" (19mm). The grain should be vertical. A small, 1" (25mm)-long piece of coat hanger wire should be inserted into the bottom (refer to the pattern) so the toucan can be mounted on the roof peak of the ark.

Tip
Mount the toucan to the roof peak with coat hanger wire.

Left Side

Right Side

Top

Front

Back

Basswood block: 1½" x 2" x ¾"
 (38mm x 51mm x 19mm)
Grain direction: Vertical

Paint Colors

› Black / Americana
  (body, eye base, pupils)
› School Bus Yellow / FolkArt
  (chest area)
› Turquoise / Delta Ceramcoat
  (face around eyes, irises)
› Hauser Light Green /
  Americana (bill)
› Primary Red / Americana
  (tip of bill)
› Jack O' Lantern Orange /
  Americana (bill detail)

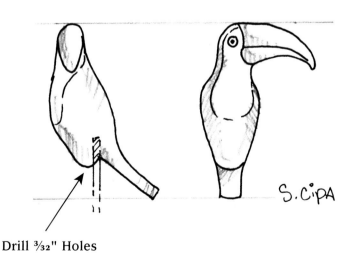

S. CiPA

Drill ³⁄₃₂" Holes

PHOTOCOPY AT 100%

Coat hangers allow the toucans to sit on the
peak of the ark's roof.

OWLS

Who? Barn owls, that's who. Use the same pattern for both genders.

Your beginning block before sawing will need to measure 1½" (38mm) wide by 1½" (38mm) high, with a thickness of ¾" (19mm). The grain should be vertical. A small, 1" (25mm)-long piece of coat hanger wire should be inserted into the bottom (refer to the pattern) so that the owl can be mounted on the roof peak of the ark.

Tip
Mount the owl to the roof peak with coat hanger wire.

Left Side

Right Side

Top

Front

Back

Basswood block: 1½" x 1½" x ¾"
(38mm x 38mm x 19mm)
Grain direction: Vertical

Paint Colors

> Snow White / Americana
(body and head)
> Light Blue / FolkArt (lowlights
for body)
> Country Twill / FolkArt (wings)
> Dark Chocolate / Americana
(feather detail)
> Black / Americana
(eye base, pupils)
> School Bus Yellow / FolkArt
(beak, irises)

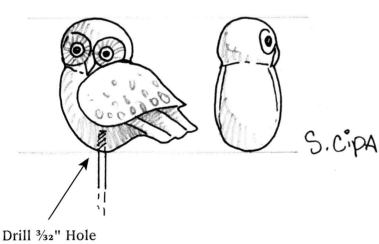

Drill ³⁄₃₂" Hole

S. CiPA

PHOTOCOPY AT 100%

Face and wing detail.

DOVES

We can't have Noah's ark without the doves! Use the same pattern for both genders.

The dove itself is carved from a block measuring 1" (25mm) wide by 1" (25mm) high with a thickness of ⅝" (16mm); however, I would strongly suggest cutting the block at least 2" (51mm) high so that you have something to hold on to when carving this extremely small project. When the dove is fully carved, simply remove the waste wood handle and fashion a flat bottom so that the dove can stand up. The grain should be vertical.

Tip
Cut the block 2" (51mm) high so you have extra wood to hold the project as you carve.

Left Side

Right Side

Top

Front

Back

Basswood block: 1" x 1" x ⅝"
(25mm x 25mm x 16mm)
Grain direction: Vertical

Paint Colors

› Snow White / Americana
(entire body)

› Light Blue / FolkArt (lowlights
for body)

› Black / Americana (dots for eyes)

› School Bus Yellow /
FolkArt (beak)

S. CiPA

PHOTOCOPY AT 100%

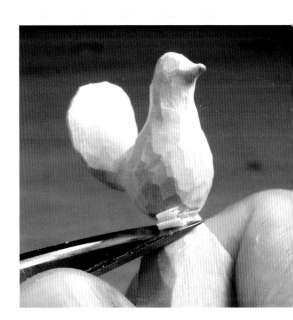

Add some extra wood to the block
measurement for the dove so you can
hold on to this small figure more easily.

BULL & COW

Basswood block: 6" x 4" x 1¾"
(152mm x 102mm x 44mm)
Grain direction: Vertical

In Old Testament times, the bull represented power, strength, and dynamic energy as supplied by God to the Israelites. Because of their symbolic meaning of strength, bulls were often found in architecture of the Old World, often holding something up or keeping something in place.

Several ancient cultures worshipped the sacred bull. The Hebrews worshipped, for a time, the idol of the golden calf created by Aaron in the wilderness of Sinai. Apis, a bull deity, was worshipped by Egyptians in the Memphis region more than 3,000 years ago. Those who follow astrology will know the bull as Taurus, the second sign of the Zodiac.

In most parts of India, the bull or cow is a sacred animal of Hindu belief, and it is strictly prohibited to slaughter or even injure the animal for any purpose. Even today the cows roam free in the streets of some major Indian cities, and it is considered to be good luck to feed one a snack before breakfast.

For this design, I chose the Brahma bull, a species originating in India and mostly recognized for the fleshy hump on its back and a large flap of skin hanging down front, known as a dewlap. Although I've included separate patterns for the bull and the cow, they are almost identical except for a few features. Most obviously, the bull possesses horns and the area from where they protrude has a bony ridge, whereas the cow has no horns and the head is more rounded off. The cow also has an udder. I mirrored the positions of the legs between the genders, and I painted them using separate color palettes.

Since this project is small, you will only need to saw the provided side pattern. It is important that the grain direction be vertical to keep the legs strong; however, the horns and ears will be extremely subject to breakage, so you will need to carve them separately and attach them into predrilled holes. The bull pattern shows two sets of ³⁄₁₆" (5mm) holes to be drilled (horns above, ears below), and the cow shows only one set for the ears. Patterns for the horns and ears have been included, and they should be cut from ³⁄₁₆" (5mm)-thick stock with the grain running horizontally. Once carved, simply glue them into place with yellow wood glue.

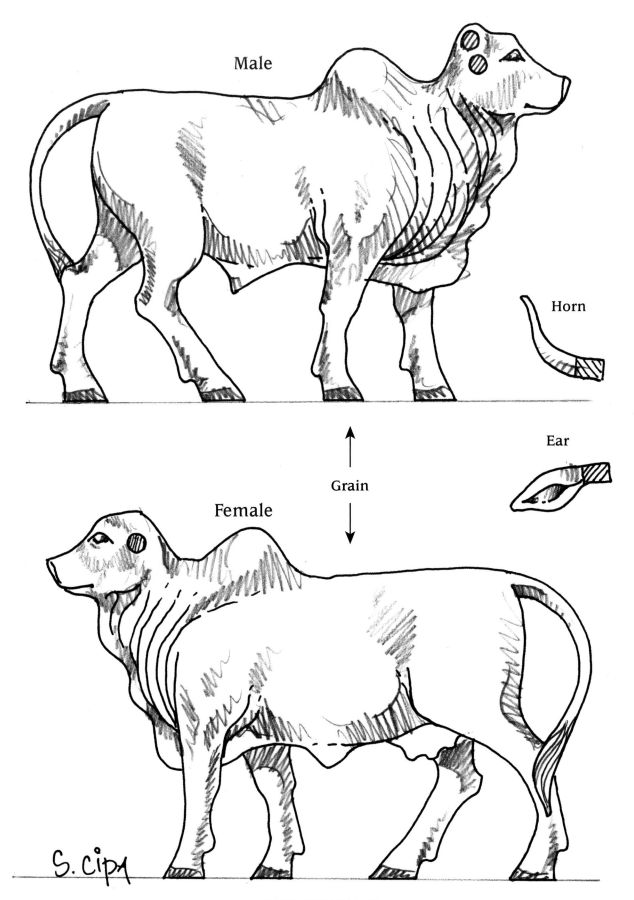

Male

Horn

Grain

Ear

Female

S. Cipa

PHOTOCOPY AT 100%

Left Side

Front   Male

Back

Right Side

Top

Female

Front

Left Side

Back

Right Side

Top

Bull head and horn details.

Cow ear and head details.

Carve the ears and horns separately and insert them into two holes drilled on each side of the bull's head.

Paint Colors: Bull

- › Linen / FolkArt (overall base color)
- › Neutral Grey / Americana (top of back, head, and tail)
- › Summer Lilac / Americana (lowlights)
- › Black / Americana (eyes, snout, hooves, wash on tips of horns, ears, hump, tip of tail)
- › Flesh / Apple Barrel (insides of ears, chin)
- › Snow White / Americana (reflective light dot on pupil)

Paint Colors: Cow

Antique White / Delta Ceramcoat (overall base color)

Country Twill / FolkArt (top of back, head, and tail)

Blue Stoneware / FolkArt (lowlights)

Black / Americana (eyes, snout, hooves, wash on tip of tail)

Flesh / Apple Barrel (insides of ears, chin, udder)

Snow White / Americana (reflective light dot on pupil)

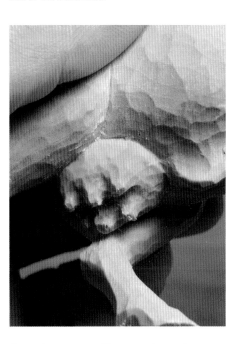

Carve the extra wood between the cow's rear legs to form the udder.

TIP
Cut the horns from separate stock. The grain should run horizontally.

ELEPHANTS

Basswood block: 7½" x 6" x 2"
(178mm x 152mm x 51mm)
Grain direction: Horizontal

Elephants are well known for their memory and in intelligence are compared to whales and primates. They are a symbol of wisdom in Asian cultures. As the largest living land animal, elephants are on the brink of extinction. Only three species of elephant remain. They cannot hide from poachers, and food sources are becoming increasingly sparse; an average adult elephant requires 300 pounds of vegetation per day in order to survive!

Medieval scholars, many who had never seen an elephant in real life, wrote of what they considered to be the elephant's primary nature: If an elephant falls down it cannot get up because it has no knee joints. For this reason, the elephant leans against a tree to sleep. A hunter partially cuts through a tree so that both the elephant and the tree crash down. But as it falls, the beast cries out loudly, and at once a large elephant arrives to help. It tries, but it cannot lift the fallen elephant. Then both cry out, and twelve more elephants heed the call. They all try, but still they cannot raise the fallen elephant. So they all cry out, and immediately a little elephant arrives and single-handedly lifts the fallen elephant. The Christian allegory to this story goes as follows: The fallen elephant represents mankind. The large elephant represents the law as recorded by Moses, which cannot raise mankind up from sin. The twelve elephants, representing the twelve prophets of the Old Testament, still cannot succeed but cry out for help. Finally, the small elephant is Christ, who succeeds in raising the fallen and abolishing sin from mankind.

My elephant design is based on the Asiatic species. It shows a trumpeting position, with the trunk lifted high. Although the same pattern is to be used for the male and the female, I mirrored the positions of the legs between the genders, and I painted them using separate color palettes. For the low lights of each, I used nontraditional colors (blue and green) to provide a folksy effect.

Since this project is small, you will only need to saw the provided side pattern. The grain direction should be horizontal to give strength to the tusks and trunk. The waste material inside the closed loop of the trunk was largely removed prior to carving with a power drill equipped with a ½" (13mm) bit.

Top View

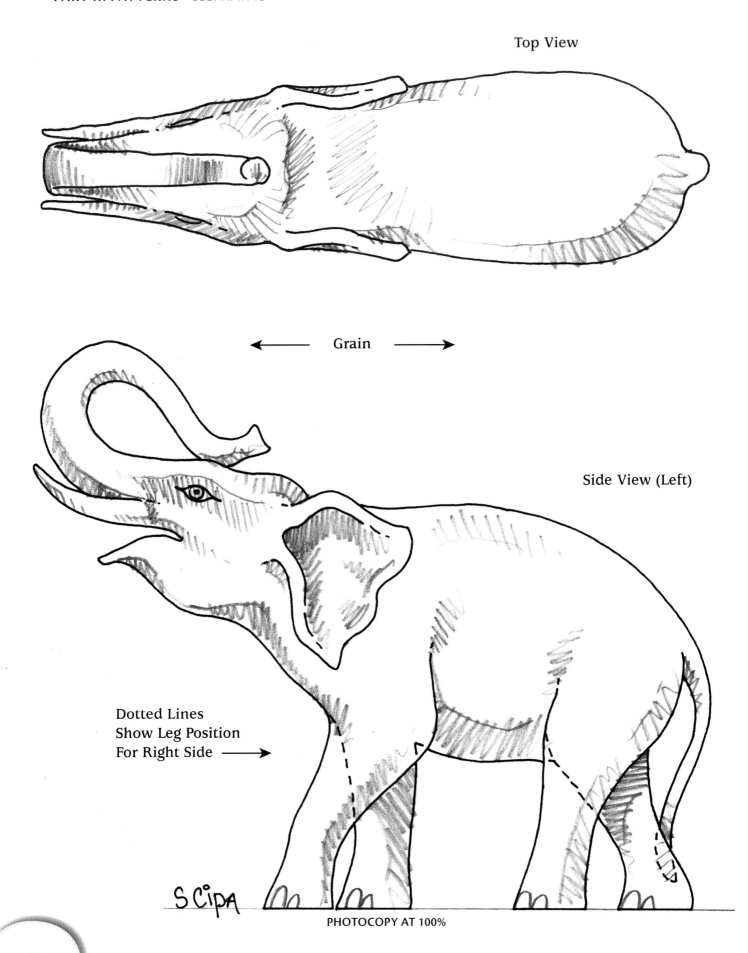

Grain

Side View (Left)

Dotted Lines
Show Leg Position
For Right Side →

SCiPA

PHOTOCOPY AT 100%

Left Side

Front   Male

Back

Right Side

Top

Front

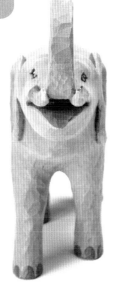

Left Side

Female

Back

Right Side

Top

Tusk and face detail.

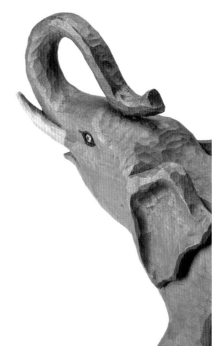

Ear and trunk details.

Paint Colors: Male

> Neutral Grey / Americana
> (overall base color)

> Blue Haze / Americana (lowlights)

> Antique White / Delta
> Ceramcoat (tusks)

> Italian Sage / FolkArt (irises,
> toe nails, shading on tusks)

> Boysenberry Pink / Americana
> (inside of mouth)

> Black / Americana
> (eye base, pupils)

> Snow White / Americana
> (reflective light dot on pupil)

Paint Colors: Female

> Sandstone / Apple Barrel
> (overall base color)

> Celery Green / Americana
> (lowlights)

> Flesh / Apple Barrel (insides
> of ears, inside of mouth)

> Neutral Grey / Americana
> (shading on tusks, toe nails)

> Village Green / Delta
> Ceramcoat (irises)

> Black / Americana
> (eye base, pupils)

> Snow White / Americana
> (reflective light dot on pupil)

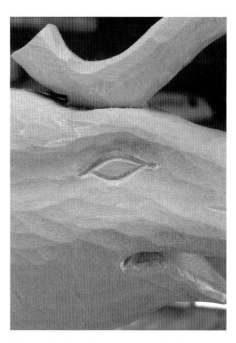

The elephant's trunk remains attached
above the eye.

Tip
Use a power drill to remove the waste
material inside the closed loop of the trunk.

FISH

Basswood block, fish (Peter):
2¾" x 1¾" x ¾" (70mm x 44mm x 19mm)

Basswood block, fish (Paul):
4¼" x 1½" x ¾" (108mm x 38mm x 19mm)

Basswood block, wave: 2½" x 1¼" x 1" (64mm x 32mm x 25mm)

Grain direction for fish and wave: Horizontal

The fish has often been used as a religious symbol in different cultures. In Christianity, it is a symbol for baptism. A fish in its natural state is totally submersed, yet does not drown. In fact, a fish must be immersed in order to survive and thus became an appropriate symbol for early Christians. As the first believers were increasingly persecuted by the local non-Christian Roman authorities, they adopted the fish symbol as a secret code so the faithful could identify each other without raising suspicion.

Although fish, as well as all other marine life, were not actually on the ark, I thought it would add interest to the project to include them. As the floodwaters rose, undoubtedly most sea creatures were destroyed due to the violent nature of the subterranean volcanic activity, but obviously some did survive to repopulate the world's oceans. Consider the thousands of extinct marine species we have found in the form of fossils!

I have provided two different fish patterns (one named Peter and the other named Paul) and carved one of each for the overall project; however, you may carve as many as you wish and place them randomly around the ark while it is on display. The shorter fish, Peter, is carved from a blank measuring 2¾" (70mm) wide by 1¾" high (44mm) by ¾" (19mm) thick. The longer fish, Paul, is carved from a blank measuring 4¼" (108mm) wide by 1½" (38mm) high by ¾" (19mm) thick. Both are mounted on a sea wave base that is carved from a blank measuring 2½" (64mm) wide by 1¼" high (32mm) by 1" (25mm) thick. Connect the fish to the base by drilling ³⁄₁₆" (5mm) holes in each to accommodate 2" (51mm)-long pieces of coat hanger wire; glue the wire in place with cyanoacrylate adhesive.

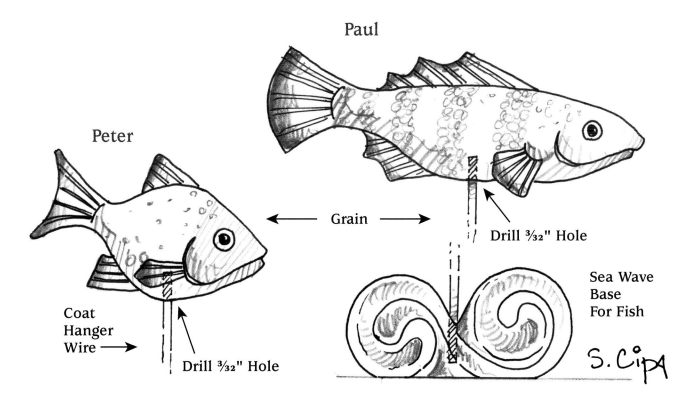

Paul

Peter

Grain

Drill ³⁄₃₂" Hole

Coat
Hanger
Wire →

Drill ³⁄₃₂" Hole

Sea Wave
Base
For Fish

S. Cipa

PHOTOCOPY AT 100%

Paint Colors: Sea Wave Base

> Light Blue / FolkArt
> Village Green / Delta Ceramcoat
> Snow White / Americana

Paint Colors: Peter

> Light Avocado / Americana (face, scale details)
> School Bus Yellow / FolkArt (body)
> Autumn Leaves / JoAnn Craft Essentials (belly, scale details)
> Antique White / Delta Ceramcoat (fins)
> Black / Americana (eye base, pupils, tips of fins)
> 14K Gold / Delta Ceramcoat (irises)
> Snow White / Americana (reflective light dot on pupil)

Paint Colors: Paul

> Autumn Leaves / JoAnn Craft Essentials (face, scale details)
> School Bus Yellow / FolkArt (body)
> Snow White / Americana (scale details, reflective light dot on pupil)
> Antique White / Delta Ceramcoat (fins)
> Bayberry / FolkArt (tips of fins)
> Black / Americana (eye base, pupils, tips of fins)
> Silver / DecoArt (irises)

Tip
Use coat hanger wire to attach the fish to the wave.

Front

Back

Top

Left Side

Right Side

HOUSE CATS

Basswood block, Hedy: 1⅝" x 1⅞" x ¾" (41mm x 48mm x 19mm)

Basswood block, Tom: 2¼" x 1½" x ¾" (57mm x 38mm x 19mm)

Grain direction for both cats: Horizontal

I have provided two separate patterns for our resident house cat pair. They have been designed to be mounted permanently or semipermanently to the ark itself.

The first one, named Hedy, sleeps curled up in one of the cabin's portholes. Referring to the pattern, notice how the piece is designed: Hedy's tail and part of her face hang down over the porthole opening, flush against the outer wall, while the main part of her body is shaped in a semicircular fashion so that she fits snugly in the porthole opening. The blank for Hedy before carving needs to measure 1⅝" (41mm) wide by 1⅞" (48mm) high by ¾" (19mm) thick. The parts hanging over will be ¼" (6mm) thick, while the remaining ½" (13mm) portion should fit flush within the opening.

The second house cat, named Tom, is designed to sit atop the yellow ledge of the Ark's cabin in close proximity to Hedy. Tom sports the same features, but his tail and paws hang over the edge. The blank for Tom before carving needs to measure 2¼" (57mm) wide by 1½" high (38mm) by ¾" (19mm) thick. The parts hanging over will be ¼" (6mm) thick, while the remaining ½" (13mm) portion should fit flush on top of the ledge.

Both cats can be permanently glued in place; however, if you wish to have to have the option of moving them around, I would suggest using Mini-Hold, a soft, tacky wax substance that is used to temporarily affix miniatures, such as dollhouse furniture, into place. Do not let them sit in place without any aid; they may fall and get damaged!

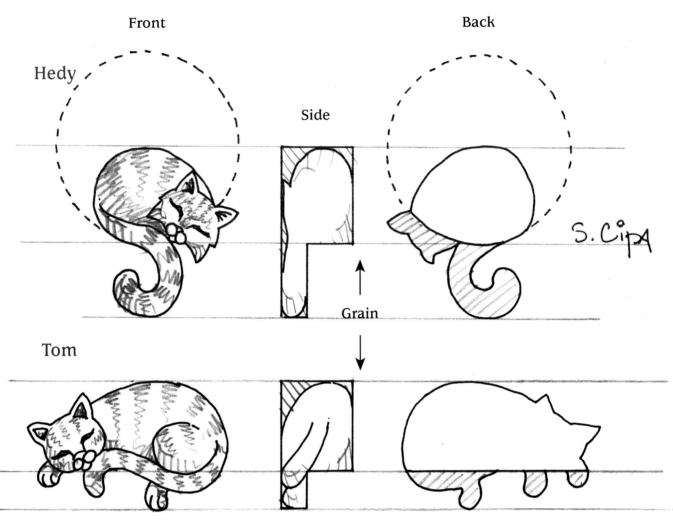

Front

Back

Hedy

Side

S. Cipa

Tom

Grain

PHOTOCOPY AT 100%

Paint Colors: Hedy

> Dark Chocolate / Americana (overall base for body)
> Black / Americana (striping detail)
> Antique White / Delta Ceramcoat (facial details)
> Flesh / Apple Barrel (nose, insides of ears)

Paint Colors: Tom

> Antique Gold / Americana (overall base for body)
> Jack O' Lantern Orange / Americana (lowlights for body)
> Rookwood Red / Americana (stripe details)
> Antique White / Delta Ceramcoat (facial details, paws)
> Flesh / Apple Barrel (nose, insides of ears)

The back side of each cat is shaped to fit inside the porthole (shown here) and on the ledge.

Tip
Use a soft, tacky wax to temporarily hold the cats in place inside the portholes.

Left Side

Right Side

Front

Top

Back

Hedy's paint detail.

GIRAFFES

Basswood block, male:
  6" x 9" x 1¾" (152mm x 229mm x 44mm).

Basswood block, female:
  4½" x 6" x 1¾" (114mm x 152mm x 44mm)

Grain direction for both giraffes: Vertical

When painting, follow these tips:

› Apply the faded washes of Antique White to the forelegs and around the eyes as well as the wash of Black to the muzzle, horns, ears, and tip of the tail before painting the spots.

› When painting the spots, apply them to the bare basswood color (no base color), leaving the natural wood tint to serve as the in-between lines.

› If you can, apply the spots freehand; pencil guidelines would surely mar the final effect.

› Practice on scrap wood.

Symbolic of attributes such as grace and farsightedness, the giraffe was originally known in Medieval Europe as the Camelopard (a cross between a camel and a leopard) and was first seen by Europeans in Rome when Caesar presented circuses to the public.

The giraffe is the tallest living land-dwelling animal; males can grow as tall as 18 feet. Giraffes don't require much sleep; they get on the average 10 minutes to 2 hours every 24 hours. They can run very fast—up to 55 miles per hour—and can fend off their only predator, the lion, with a powerful kick.

When I started researching giraffes in order to create a design for this book, I realized how unusual their anatomy is. I actually struggled with it for a while, until something finally clicked into place. They have humps and bumps in strange places, but they are a perfect example of form and function working together in harmony.

The subspecies of giraffe I chose to base my design on is the reticulated giraffe, which refers to the shape of its spots. The spots are polygonal, meaning they have multiple sides to them, as opposed to a circular shape. Upon studying photos of giraffes, I noticed that the reticulated variety possesses polygon shapes containing three to five sides in an irregular fashion. The shapes are largest on the back and neck, and get smaller and closer together toward the head and legs, eventually fading out.

I designed a second pattern for the female, but you can certainly choose to carve both standing or both sitting. The painting scheme is the same for both genders.

Even though the male is one of the larger projects in this book, it's thickness is still only 1¾" (44mm). You will only need to saw the provided side pattern image. It is extremely important that the grain direction be vertical so that the legs and neck can remain strong. The base is a randomly shaped piece of wood that connects all four feet and improves stability since the male's legs are so long. The waste material inside the closed areas between the legs was largely removed prior to carving with a scroll saw.

Saw only the side pattern image for the seated giraffe. Use the front pattern image as a reference when shaping the head profile.

Male

Grain

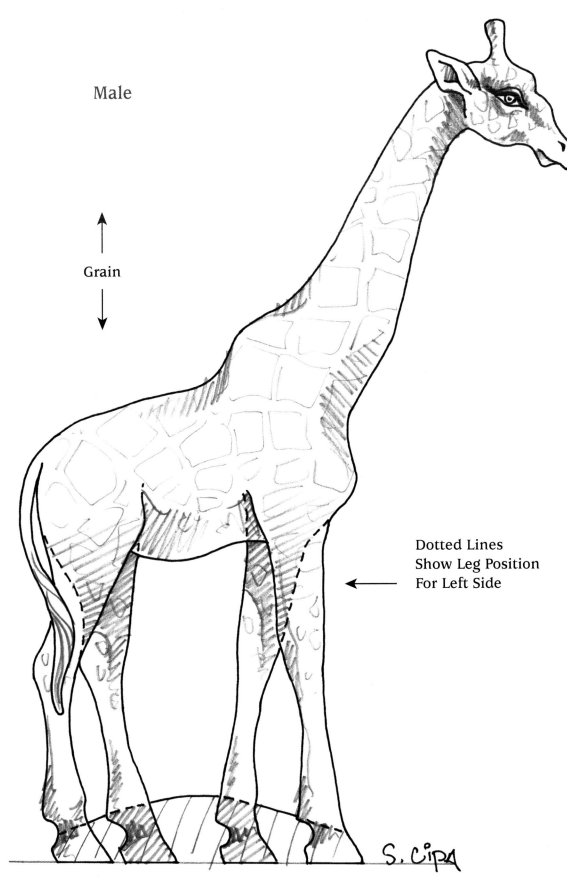

Dotted Lines
Show Leg Position
For Left Side

S. Cipa

PHOTOCOPY AT 100%

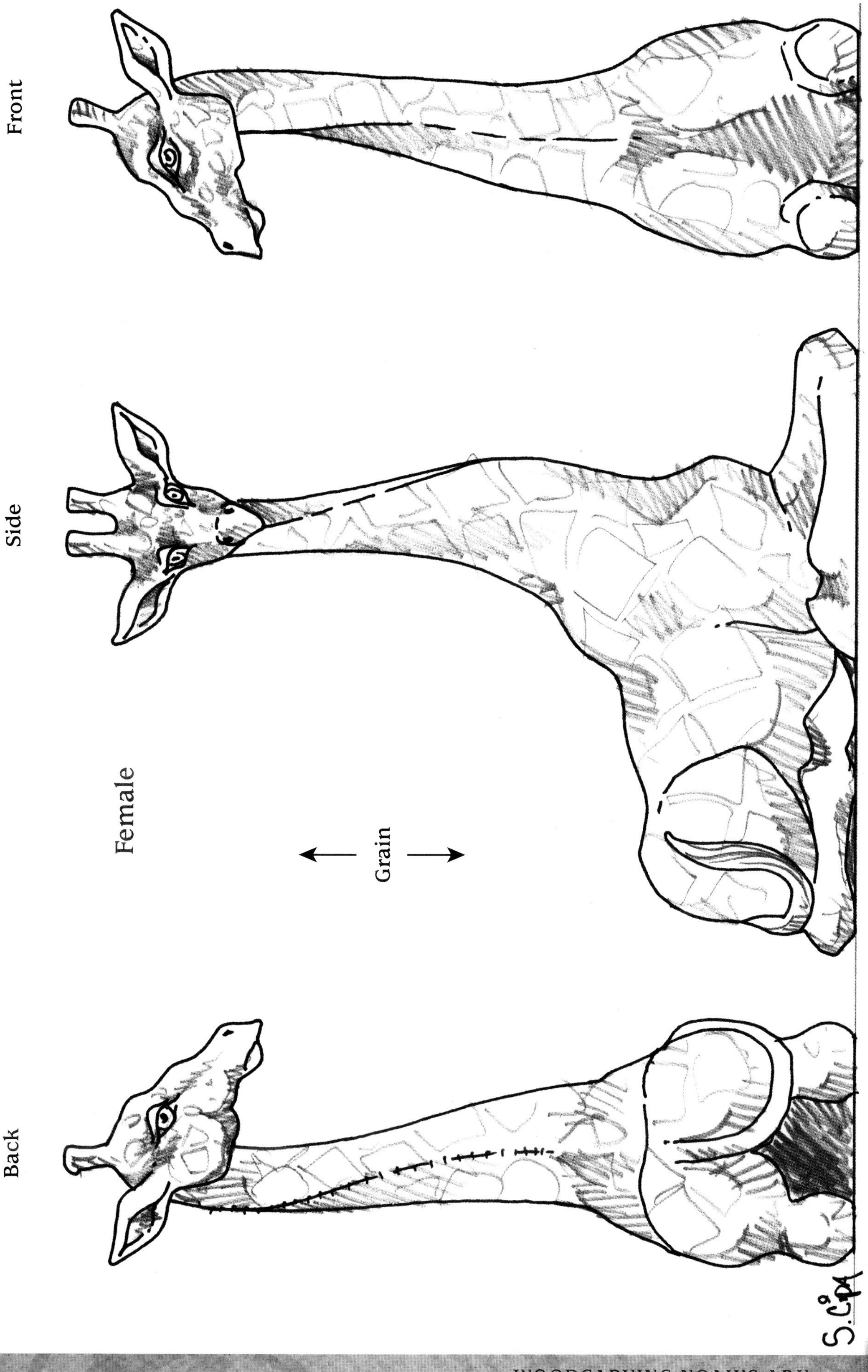

Front

Side

Back

Female

← Grain →

PHOTOCOPY AT 100%

Front

Left Side

Right Side

Male

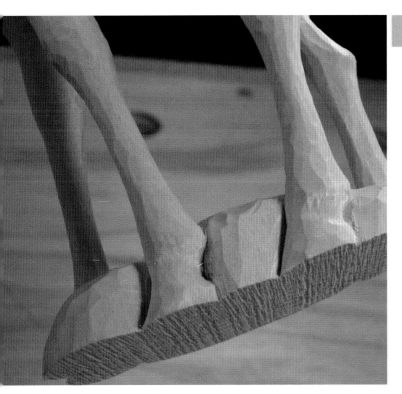

Back

Top

The giraffe's legs are carved as part of the base to give more support to this long-legged creature.

Right Side

Left Side Female

Back

Front

Top

Paint Colors: Male and Female

> Rookwood Red / Americana (polygonal spots)
> Antique White / Delta Ceramcoat (forelegs, around the eyes)
> Country Twill / FolkArt (hooves)
> Black / Americana (muzzle, ear tips, horns, tip of tail, eye base, eye lashes, pupils)
> Raw Sienna / FolkArt (irises)
> Snow White / Americana (reflective light dot on pupils)

Tip
For both giraffes, cut the side patterns. Use the front and back female patterns for reference.

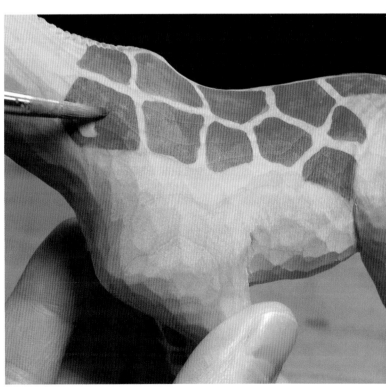

Paint the giraffe's easily recognized pattern directly on the wood.

NOAH'S WIFE

Basswood block: 2½" x 6" x 2½"
(64mm x 152mm x 64mm)
Grain direction: Vertical

Although the wife of Noah did not have a name assigned to her in the book of Genesis, Jewish texts name her as Naamah, meaning "beautiful one." Despite being mentioned only five times in Genesis (as Noah's wife), she is undoubtedly one of the most significant women in biblical history.

As Noah's spouse, she would have served God just as obediently as her husband did by being Noah's faithful helper and submitting to his leadership. She toiled alongside Noah for many years, helping him to build the ark, and she also played a large part in being "zookeeper" during the flood. Her faith must have been great to stand by his side as he was ridiculed by others and to endure the thought of what was to come.

Your beginning block before sawing Noah's Wife will need to measure 2½" (64mm) wide by 6" (152mm) high, with a thickness of 2½" (64mm). Because this project is small and only 2½" thick, you will only need to saw the provided front pattern image. The grain should run vertically.

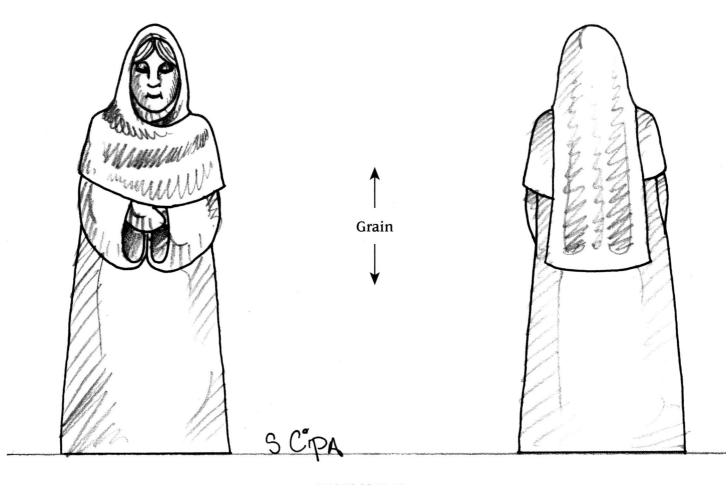

Grain

S C̊PA

PHOTOCOPY AT 100%

Tip
See the step-by-step section on carving Noah; many of the carving techniques used there can also be applied to Noah's Wife.

Front

Back

Top

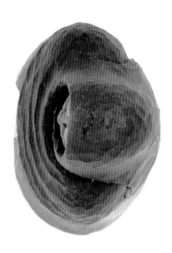

Left Side

Right Side

Paint Colors: Noah's Wife

> Country Twill / Apple Barrel (robe)
> Dark Chocolate / Americana (robe lowlights)
> Rookwood Red / Americana (shawl)
> Royal Purple / Americana (shawl lowlights)
> Neutral Grey / Americana (hair)
> Antique White / Delta Ceramcoat (hair highlights)
> Autumn Leaves / JoAnn Craft Essentials (rosy cheeks)

PIGS

Basswood block: 4" x 2" x 1¼"
(102mm x 51mm x 32mm)
Grain direction: Vertical

Pigs are very intelligent and social animals, despite being associated with gluttony and uncleanliness. It is said that pigs wallow in the mud, which makes them dirty animals, but the reason they wallow is because they have no sweat glands. Pigs cover themselves in mud to cool down and even to avoid sunburn!

Pigs have a very keen sense of smell, so much so that they have often been used to seek out truffles, a fungal delicacy found primarily at the base of trees. Dogs have been trained to seek out truffles as well, but pigs do not need training; they have an innate ability to sniff them out. Unfortunately, they also like to eat the truffles, once they find them. Interestingly, this is because the truffle contains a compound that is very similar to the sex pheromone found in boars. Hmm, who knew?

As we all know, pigs are a very popular source of food throughout the world, but certain religious groups, specifically Judaism and Islam, consider the eating of pork strictly forbidden, marking them as "unclean" animals.

My design is that of an ordinary domestic pig, otherwise known as the hog. The pattern provided is to be used for both the male and female, as they appear to be identical. I mirrored the positions of the back legs between the genders, and I painted them using separate color palettes.

Your beginning block before sawing will need to measure 4" (102mm) wide by 2" (51mm) high, with a thickness of 1¼" (32mm). Since this project is small, you will only need to saw the provided side pattern image. It is important that the grain direction be vertical so that the tiny legs can remain strong.

A centerline helps to keep the carving in perspective as you are shaping the pieces.

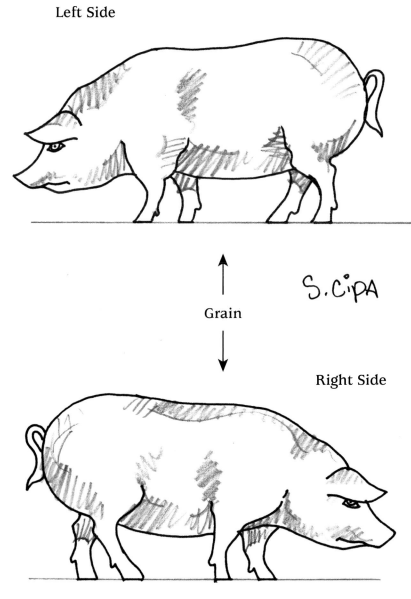

Left Side

Grain

S. CiPA

Right Side

PHOTOCOPY AT 100%

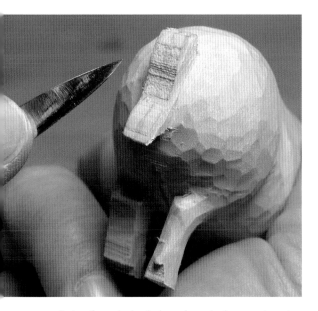

A view from the back shows how the legs are shaped and how they flow into the body.

Tip
Carve the legs of the female to mirror those of the male.

Paint Colors: Male
› Flesh / Apple Barrel (overall base color)
› Burnt Umber / FolkArt (spots)
› Black / Americana (eye base, pupils)
› Antique White / Delta Ceramcoat (irises)

Paint Colors: Female
› Boysenberry Pink / Americana (overall base color)
› Black / Americana (eye base, pupils)
› Antique White / Delta Ceramcoat (spots, irises)

Left Side

Right Side

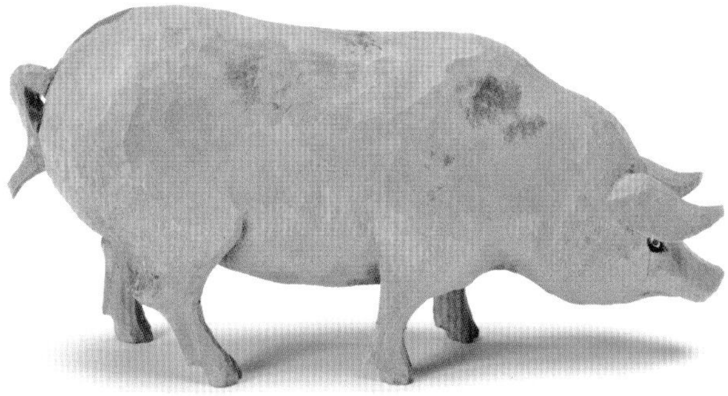

Male

Front

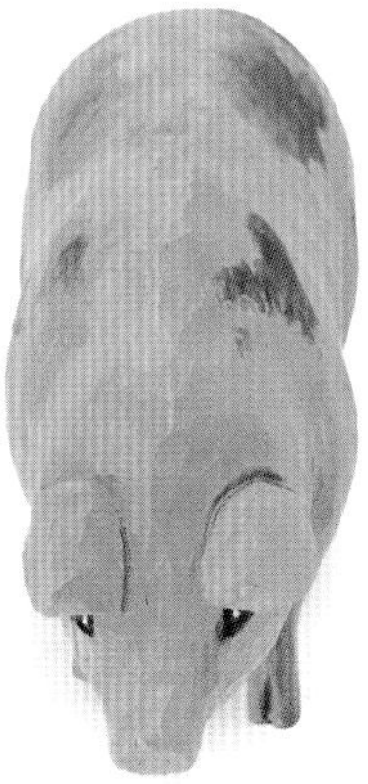

Back

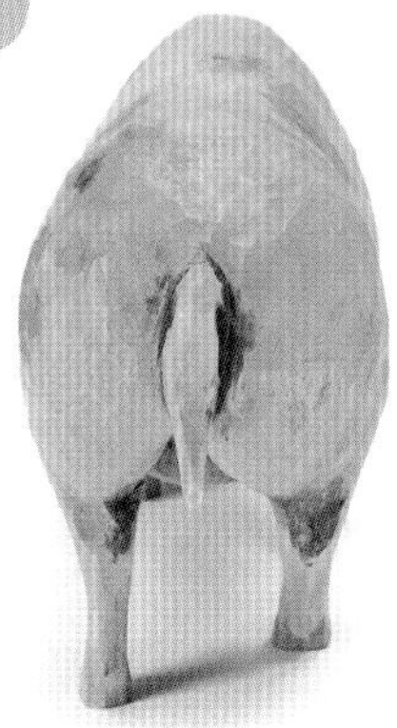

Top

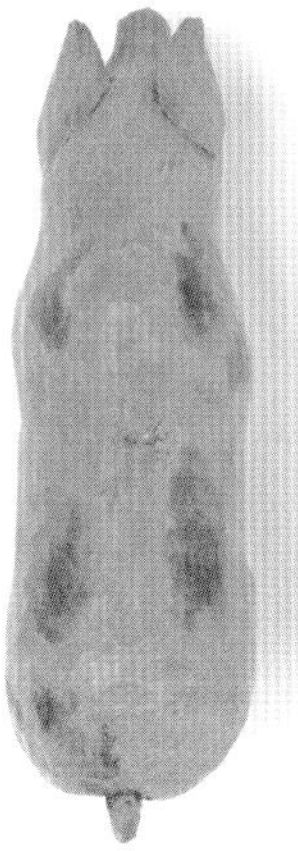

Left Side

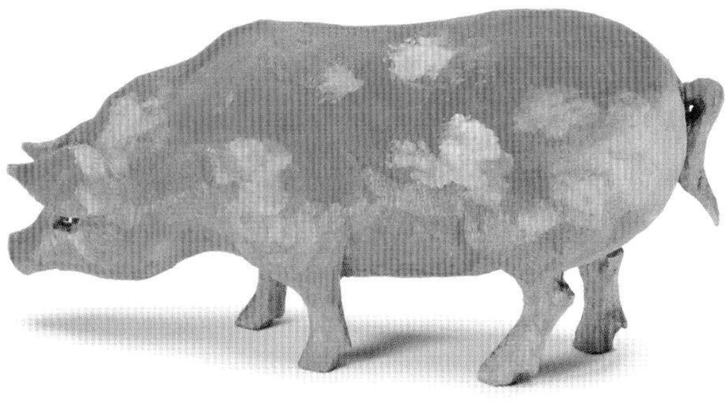

Right Side

Female

Front

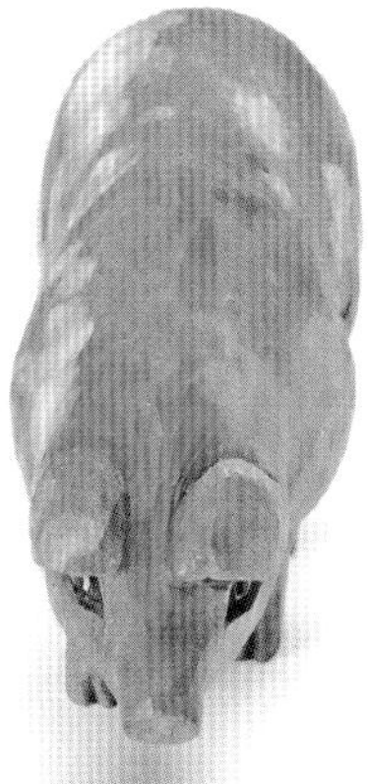

Back

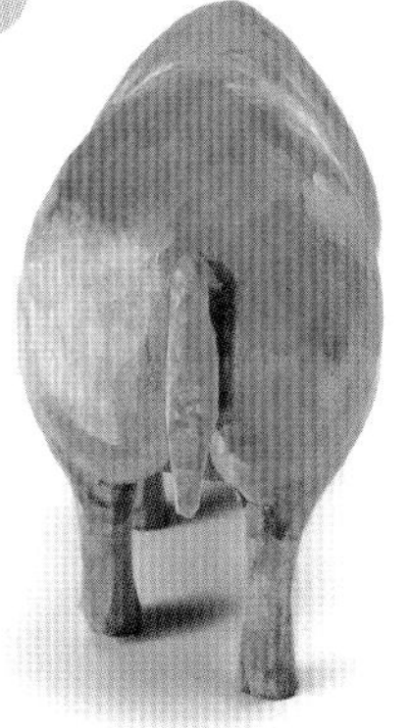

Top

SHEEP

Basswood block: 3¾" x 3" x 1½"
(95mm x 78mm x 38mm)
Grain direction: Vertical

The ram and ewe, collectively known as sheep, are deeply entrenched in human culture and have been found to be popular subjects in fables and nursery rhymes, such as "The Wolf in Sheep's Clothing," "Little Bo Peep," and "Mary Had a Little Lamb." They have also been the subject of many catch phrases, like "sheep to the slaughter," "black sheep," and "counting sheep." One can also be "sheepish."

As one of the first animals to ever be raised as domestic livestock, sheep have served several functions: wool for clothing; meat, or mutton, for food; and even dairy. Sheep were also the most desired "clean" animal for sacrificial purposes. The ancient Greeks and Romans both slaughtered sheep regularly in religious practice, and the Jews of the Old Testament did as well.

Sheep play an influential role in both the Old and New testaments as well as the Koran. Abraham, Isaac, Jacob, Moses, David, and Muhammad were all shepherds by trade. Noah was instructed by God to bring seven pairs of sheep into the ark so that he had some to sacrifice as part of a covenant to God after the flood was over.

Christians as a whole are known to be members of the flock, with Christ as the Good Shepherd. Christ himself is sometimes referred to as Angus Dei, the sacrificial lamb.

For this design, I chose the Shetland sheep as inspiration, a species originating in the Shetland Isles of Scotland. Although I created separate patterns for the ram and the ewe, they are practically identical aside from one distinctive feature: horns. The ram's horns spiral around toward the front and are close to his body. I mirrored the positions of the back legs between the genders, and I painted them using separate color palettes.

Your beginning block before sawing for both the ram and the ewe should measure 3¾" (95mm) wide by 3" (78mm) high, with a thickness of 1½" (38mm). Since this project is small, you will only need to saw the side pattern. It is important that the grain direction run vertically so the tiny legs can remain strong.

Right Side

Grain

Left Side

S.Cipa

PHOTOCOPY AT 100%

Left Side

Front Female

Back

Right Side

Top

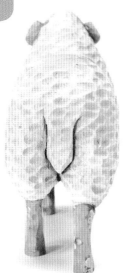

Front

Left Side

Male

Back

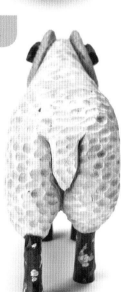

Right Side

Top

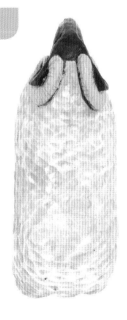

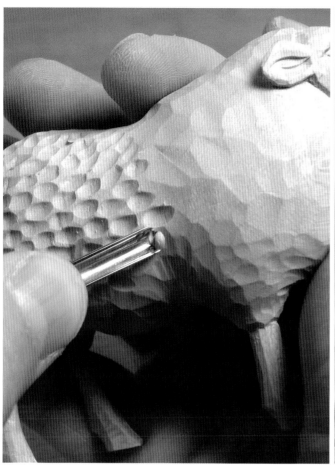

Small divots removed from the surface of the sheep will give the impression of their woolly fur.

A close-up shot of the ram's head in progress shows how the ear lies on top of the horn which lies on top of the fur.

Paint Colors: Ram

> Antique White / Delta Ceramcoat (overall base color, spots on legs, wash on muzzle)
> Black / Americana (face, legs, eye base, pupils)
> Country Twill / FolkArt (horns)
> Raw Sienna / FolkArt (lowlights, irises)

Paint Colors: Ewe

> Antique White / Delta Ceramcoat (overall base color, spots on legs and face)
> Country Twill / FolkArt (base color for face and legs)
> Blue Stoneware / FolkArt (lowlights)
> Black / Americana (eye base, pupils, nose)
> Flesh / Apple Barrel (insides of ears)
> Dark Chocolate / Americana (spots on legs and face)
> Raw Sienna / FolkArt (irises)

Ram's horn and face detail.

Tip

Take extra care when carving the curved horns of the ram.

PART II: PATTERNS

WHALE

Basswood block: 10" x 5" x ½"
(254mm x 127mm x 64mm)
Grain direction: Horizontal

As the largest animal ever known to exist, the whale has received more awe and wonder than any other animal on the face of the earth. It comes as no surprise then that cultural mythology surrounds this elusive creature of the depths. Because they spend 90 percent of their lives underwater, the whale has been little understood for most of human history.

In Medieval bestiaries, it was said that whales remained floating on the surface for long periods of time, so long that sand would settle on their backs. Passing sailors would mistake the whale for a small island, anchor there, start cook fires, and even stake their ship to the sandy surface. Once the whale sensed the burning upon its back, it plunged down into the depths to cool off. The sailors, ship and all, were also dragged down to their death. The Christian allegory to this story indicates that the whale

is like the devil, deceiving man and dragging him into the depths of hell.

Another supposed nature of the whale was that when hungry, it opened its mouth, emitting a sweet odor. Small fish were attracted to the odor and swam into the whale's mouth; the whale then closed its jaws down upon them. The moral here is that men of weak faith (the small fish) who are lured by the sweet scent of worldly desires will be devoured by the devil, again portrayed by the whale.

These decidedly dark themes are in stark contrast to the true nature of whales, which are largely docile and quite intelligent.

My whale design is that of a blue whale, the largest animal currently on the planet. Blue whales are classified as baleen whales because of the comblike baleen that they have in place of teeth. This bony structure filters small marine animals from mouthfuls of sea water.

Technically, the whale is not one of Noah's animals, as it did not need the ark to survive. However, I could not resist adding one into the mix (I did not carve a pair). The whale can be placed around the outside of the ark, along with the fish also found in this book. The design shows the whale's body partially hidden within the stylized, folk art waves, with the tail emerging straight up. This position gives the impression that his belly is below

PHOTOCOPY AT 100%

Grain

S. Cipa

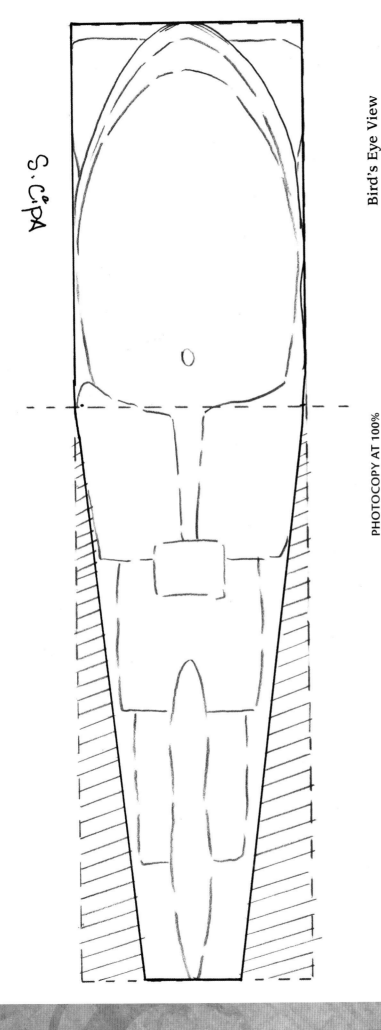

S. Cipa

Bird's Eye View

PHOTOCOPY AT 100%

the surface. Please take note that a whale's tail fin is actually horizontal in relationship to its body; however, I have used artistic license and placed it vertically like a fish in interest of the design. If this rendering does not sit well with you, by all means, modify the design.

Your beginning block before sawing should measure 10" (254mm) wide by 5" (127mm) high, with a thickness of 2½" (64mm). Although this project is the largest carving project in the book, you will still only need to saw the side pattern, with one exception: after sawing the side image, saw the overall shape into a rough wedge (see the bird's eye view pattern on this page). From the front head area to the tip of the whale's flippers (about 4" [102mm]), the blank should remain at the full 2½" (64mm) width then taper toward the tail evenly on both sides to end at about 1" (25mm) thick at the tail. This cut does not have to be exact, but it will help to remove a great deal of waste in a hurry. The grain direction can run horizontally for this project.

I used thin, light pencil lines to mark the whale's baleen, and I stippled the sea waves with White to suggest froth.

Front

Left Side

Back

Right Side

Top

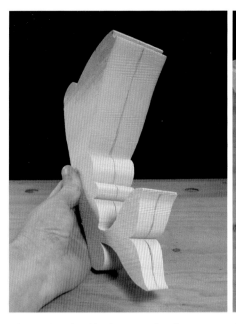

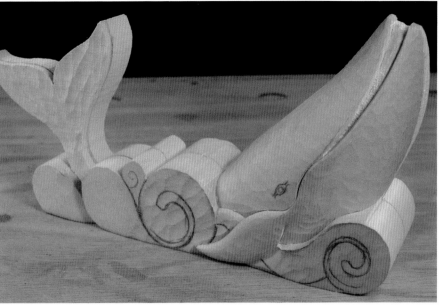

After cutting the side view, use a band saw to taper the top so the whale's shape is wedgelike.

Sharply defined lines between the whale's body and the water will make it appear as if the whale is emerging from the waves.

Eye, blowhole, and wave detail.

Paint Colors: Whale

> Blue Stoneware / Apple Barrel (overall base coat, except for the underbelly)
> Blue Haze / Americana (lowlights to be used with the Blue Stoneware)
> Trail Tan / Delta Ceramcoat (base color for underbelly)
> Dove Grey / Americana (lowlights for underbelly)
> Black / Americana (eye base, pupils)
> Neutral Grey / Americana (irises)
> Snow White / Americana (spots for underbelly, reflective light dot on pupils)

Paint Colors: Sea Waves

> Light Blue / FolkArt
> Village Green / Delta Ceramcoat
> Snow White / Americana

Tip

After sawing the side profile, cut the top profile in a wedge shape to remove excess waste wood.

IN THE
BEGINNING

THE STORY BEHIND NOAH'S ARK

The story of Noah and the Great Flood that I'm most familiar with is found in the Bible, Genesis chapters 6 through 9. In it, God saw how great wickedness had become and decided to wipe mankind from the face of the earth. However, one righteous man among all the people of that time found favor in God's eyes. His name was Noah. With very specific instructions, God told Noah to build an ark for him and his family (Noah's wife and his three sons and their wives) in preparation for a catastrophic flood that would destroy every living thing on earth.

God also instructed Noah to bring into the ark two (and in some cases seven) of all living creatures, male and female, along with every kind of food for the animals and his family while on the ark. Noah obeyed everything God commanded him to do.

After they entered the ark, it rained for a period of 40 days and nights, and underground waters also burst forth. The waters flooded the earth for 150 days, and every living thing on the face of the earth was wiped out. As the waters receded, the ark came to rest on the mountains of Ararat. Noah and his family continued to wait for almost eight more months while the surface of the earth dried out.

Finally after an entire year, God invited Noah to come out of the ark. Immediately, Noah built

Noah's ark sets were often carved and constructed for children as biblical teaching toys as early as the 1700s, and they became popular during the Victorian era of the nineteenth century. Victorian parents of wealthy families believed that games should not be played on Sundays, due to the strict observance of the Sabbath. Their

Noah sends a dove from the ark. Miniature on vellum at the Museum Meermanno Westreenianum, The Hague. From Aegidius of Roya's Compendium historiae universalis.

children, however, were allowed to play with Noah's ark sets and other biblically themed toys, such as nativities. Noah's ark toys were at first only found in the wealthiest of Victorian homes and were popular as gifts at Christmastime. Simpler sets were eventually made, often by the families themselves, and their popularity spread throughout Europe and to the American pioneer west.

The quality of ark sets at the time varied greatly, as did the style. Some were flat-bottomed designs, which consisted mainly of a house built upon a flat deck, lacking a hull. Others were full-bodied ships with storage compartments. Most were made individually by hand and constructed of wood and tin pieces held together by tacks and hot bone glue; stenciled designs were often applied. The selection of animals also varied greatly. Typically, the maker included 10 to 17 pairs of animals, but some made up to 50.

an altar and worshiped the Lord with burnt offerings from some of the animals. God was pleased with the offerings and promised never again to destroy all the living creatures as he had just done. Later God established a covenant with Noah: "Never again will there be a flood to destroy the earth." As a sign of this everlasting covenant, God set a rainbow in the clouds.

The Ark that Noah Built

Although the purpose of this book is to provide a fun and creative project derived from folk art origins, I must note that the ark represented in this book in no way even remotely resembles the actual working ark that Noah built under specific instruction.

Let's take a look at some actual ark logistics.

SIZE. According to Genesis 6:15–16, God gave Noah very specific measurements in cubits—a cubit is about 18" (457mm). The measurements were 300 cubits long, 50 cubits wide, and 30 cubits high; that is 450' (137m) by 75' (23m) by 45' (14m). God also instructed that the ark should have a 1-cubit (18" [457mm]) opening below the roof all the way around, presumably a window for ventilation and light; a door on the side for entry; and three stories or levels. Basically, the ark was a large rectangular vessel. It may have had a rounded bow and stern, but the Bible doesn't give those specifics. It was exactly six times longer than it was wide—the same ratio used by modern ship builders. As a point of interest, wooden sailing ships never got much longer than about 330' (100m) in the Western

Noah's Ark mosaic from Notre-Dame de la Garde, Marseille, France.

My ark design was inspired by nineteenth century hand-carved and painted Noah's ark sets, similar to this set, which has more than 50 carved animals and measures 12" (305mm) high and 24" (610m) long. Photo courtesy of Yew Tree House Antiques, www.yewtreehouseantiques.com.

Neo-Assyrian clay tablet of the Epic of Gilgamesh, Tablet 11: Story of the Flood. Known as the "Flood Tablet."

world, but the ancient Greeks built vessels at least the size of the ark 2,000 years earlier.

MATERIALS. Genesis 6:14 states that the ark was to be made of gopher wood, have compartments (stalls and rooms), and covered inside and out with pitch. What is gopher wood? We don't really know. Gopher was translated from a Hebrew word, and no such tree exists today. Many biblical translations refer to different species, such as cypress, cedar, and acacia. Other research implies that gopher referred to the manner or method used to prepare the wood. Some translations suggest the

word to mean squared beams or laminated wood.

Pitch refers to bitumen, which is an organic, naturally occurring tarlike form of petroleum. Pitch was used to waterproof the ark.

We know that Noah had the help of his three sons, Shem, Ham, and Japheth, in building the ark; he may have had more. We don't know how long it took to build, but biblical timelines suggest no more than 100 to 120 years.

SO MANY ANIMALS. When we think of how many species of animals exist today, the question that begs to be asked is how did they all fit. Several points must be considered in order to determine the feasibility of the ark's capacity. First, according to Genesis 6:19–20, God ordered Noah to bring "two of every sort . . . according to their kind" of animal, male and female. The word "kind" is the key here: the tremendous variety in species we see today did not exist in the days of Noah. Only the "parents" of these species were needed to repopulate the earth. For example, more than 200 breeds of dogs exist today, all which have descended from one original dog kind. The genetic information stored within that original kind made it possible to breed all the wonderful variations we have today. When applying the concept to all other species, the number of animals that needed to

be on the ark is greatly reduced. Also, Noah would have most likely been presented with younger animals; since they weren't fully grown, Noah would have needed even less space. The ark only needed to carry air-breathing, land-dwelling animals. This consideration also reduced the numbers that needed to be on board.

All in all, the total estimates vary according to kinds; however, a rough estimate shows that as few as 2,000 animals may have been needed, and there was certainly room on the ark for at least twice that many.

FLOOD STORIES FROM OTHER CULTURES

Many other cultures have their own flood or deluge theories apart from the biblical version; some are quite detailed, while others are more obscure. Although variances occur from story to story, most share the same basic concept: the earth was intentionally destroyed by a higher authoritative power and, afterward, was repopulated by a chosen few.

Let's take a look at some of the more prevalent stories.

ISLAM. The Qur'an's version of the flood story is similar to the Old Testament's Genesis version but with some interesting variations. Noah (or Nuh), being one of Islam's five principle prophets, is depicted as preaching and giving much warning to those who were worshipping idols instead of submitting to Allah (God). Allah then sent the flood to punish those who would not listen. Some conflicting interpretation exists here as to whether the flood was local rather than global.

Noah was accompanied by 70 to 80 voyagers, including family members. However, one of his sons refused to board the ark, wishing to take his chances on a mountaintop. Despite Noah's pleading with Allah, his son went his own way and drowned. After the flood, the ark rested upon Mount Judi.

Several contemporaries of the prophet Muhammad added some color to the story with interpretative embellishments. One wrote that Noah was unsure of what shape the ark should be, so Allah instructed that it was to be like a "bird's belly" and constructed of teakwood. Noah then planted a single tree that grew for 20 years and provided him with all the required lumber!

Another writer recorded that the ark was 300 cubits (the same size as the Genesis ark), complete with three levels, and that every single plank had the name of a prophet engraved on it. After the flood, Allah commanded the earth to absorb all the water. Certain areas were not "obedient," so Allah cursed the water with salt as punishment. Today's oceans are meant to be the remaining unabsorbed, original floodwaters.

BABYLON. This flood story is actually a small part of a much larger, ancient writing called the *Epic of Gilgamesh*. Gilgamesh was a hero-king who underwent an extensive quest, eventually seeking immortality. He heard of a man named Utnapishtim (Noah) who had been granted eternal life by the gods. Gilgamesh then sought out Utnapishtim to find out how he, too, could be made immortal. Once Gilgamesh found him, Utnapishtim told him the story of the Great Flood.

After being displeased with the human race, the gods decided to destroy humankind and with it all living things. Ea, the god of wisdom, who favored Utnapishtim, warned him of the coming flood and taught him how to construct a huge vessel in which his family and the seed of every living creature might escape. The boat was to be as tall as it was wide (660' by 660' [201m by 201m]). The flood came and went, and it was so terrible that it even frightened the gods. After witnessing the destruction, the gods regretted their decision and vowed never again to destroy humankind. After making a sacrifice to the gods, Utnapishtim and his wife were rewarded with eternal life.

The Epic of Gilgamesh has many more details, but in the end, the tale's hero never received eternal life and realized that it would be his heroic deeds that would, in a sense, give him immortality.

Islamic miniature featuring the ark.

INDIA. In Hindu tradition, the first human was named Manu, the father of all mankind. Manu was endowed with great wisdom and was devoted to virtue. One day while washing his hands in a river, a small fish jumped into his hand (the fish was an incarnation of Vishnu, or Supreme God) and begged Manu to spare his life. Moved by compassion, Manu put the fish in his water jar, but the fish soon outgrew it. He then placed him in a pitcher. After outgrowing the pitcher, he moved the fish to a well. When the well proved to be too small, he placed the fish in a tank. As the fish continued to grow, it was moved to a river and eventually the ocean. Still the fish grew and nearly filled the expanse of the entire ocean.

At this time, the fish warned Manu of a worldwide deluge that would destroy all life. Manu then built a huge boat in order to house his family, nine types of seeds, and animals to repopulate the earth when the waters receded. After the flood, Manu's boat came to rest on top of the Malaya Mountains.

CARVING AND PAINTING
BASICS

Before you begin any project, it's a good idea to review the basic skills required to get a feel for the materials you'll be using. You'll be using basic carving cuts, such as push and pull cuts with a knife, and stop cuts and chip cuts to remove wood. I've also used gouges and veiners where these specialized tools make the job easier. Knowledge of how to operate a scroll saw and/or band saw is important for cutting the carving blanks and for constructing the ark.

In addition to the carving and woodworking basics, you'll want to be familiar with some other materials. I glue up pieces with wood glue, cyanoacrylate (instant) glue, or hot glue as needed. All of the projects are painted with acrylics, finished with a satin polyurethane finish, and antiqued with brown wood gel. My goal is to create an ark inspired by 19th century Noah's ark toys but give it a folk art twist.

PREPARING THE BLANK

The first step in carving any piece is preparing the wood blank. Starting with a piece of wood properly sized for the project you're carving is vital to reducing the amount of time spent getting rid of excess material.

Wood choice

Basswood is probably the most common and popular carving wood in the United States, and I used it for all the carvings in this book. It is soft enough to carve comfortably but hard enough to hold great detail. It has virtually no grain to speak of, which makes it ideal for painting.

If you choose not to paint your Noah's ark figures, several other species of wood are ideal for the projects in this book. Hardwoods such as black walnut, cherry, and maple are very attractive, needing nothing more than a good oil finish. However, these three species in particular are considerably hard and difficult to carve. Unless you are already familiar with carving these types of wood, I would suggest practicing with basswood first.

Butternut and mahogany, although considered hardwoods, are easy to carve. Butternut is particularly soft and has a very prominent and handsome grain. Mahogany carves wonderfully and has a beautiful natural color. These two woods are best finished with some type of varnish.

Using patterns

You will want to photocopy the patterns from this book and use them as templates. All of the patterns are actual size, so they do not need to be enlarged. Cut out the pattern, and trace it on the block of wood you have prepared. Because the figures are all drawn at a considerably small scale and because the wood stock is 2" (51mm) thick or less, you do

not need to trace patterns for multiple sides. Use the main pattern for tracing; the additional pattern drawings (when included) are for reference only.

Grain direction

Be sure to coordinate the pattern properly with the grain. The grain direction is marked on the pattern pages. Getting the grain direction correct is crucial because most of the animals are very small and have tiny legs, which means the grain must run the length of the legs. Otherwise, these delicate appendages will easily snap off.

Sawing the blank

The dimensions for the wood blanks are noted for each project.

Most of the project patterns in this book are fairly simple to band saw; however, if you are new to band sawing, don't be intimidated or discouraged. Just take your time and plan your cut before plunging in. Be sure to cut out small bites at a time and to leave extra wood around small protrusions. Practicing on scrap wood first will certainly help, if you feel the need.

Do not use a blade wider than ¼" (6mm) to saw the patterns. Some of the smaller projects could even be sawed with a scroll saw,

Basswood is ideal for these projects because it is easy to carve and shows the cut marks on the finished pieces, which helps to heighten the handmade, folk art feel of each piece.

if available. Of course, if you do not feel comfortable sawing some of these patterns, have a more experienced person do it for you. Always remember to wear goggles and practice safety at all times!

Using a vise

Some of the carving projects such as the elephants, lions, and giraffes, will need to be clamped at the beginning stages in order to block out the legs.

Using a variety of gouges, V-tools, and speciality knives can make it easier to carve certain areas of each piece, such as the waste wood between the legs or the hair on a lion's mane.

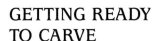

Your favorite carving knife can be used to carve the projects in this book.

Any carver's vise or clamping system will do. I use a simple carpenter's vise that is built into my workbench. I combine it with bench dogs to wedge the project in place. If you will be using a common machine vise, be sure to line the inside of the jaws with some thin pieces of basswood; anything harder and the carving will become marred. After blocking out the figure, you will be able to hold the pieces by hand while you carve them.

GETTING READY TO CARVE

As far as most of the projects in this book are concerned, the tool requirements are moderate. My personal course of action for these projects is as follows: While the carving is in a vise, rough out the blank with a larger shallow gouge and possibly a mallet. Switch to medium-sized gouges and a variety of knives to work the piece into shape. Apply details with small palm gouges and more knife work.

A sharp tool is essential. You might think this goes without saying, but so many beginners struggle with a piece of wood only to give up in frustration. They blame themselves, thinking they don't have what it takes, when all along a dull tool is the culprit. To carve with the sharpest of tools is a joy that must be experienced to be appreciated.

I suggest purchasing a good sharpening book from your local or mail order carving supply store if you are not already accustomed to sharpening your own tools successfully.

Wood softener

Sometimes basswood is not as soft as it should be. Sometimes the grade isn't so great, but it's all you've got. Sometimes you have a lot of detail to carve right into the end grain, and no matter how sharp your tool is, it still seems to tear the fibers instead of slicing through them. In these cases, you need a wood softener.

To make wood softener, prepare a 50/50 mixture of water and isopropyl alcohol, put it in a spray or mister bottle, and spray it lightly on the area being worked. Let it soak in for a few moments, and spray it again. Now start carving! The tool should glide through the stubborn wood much easier.

Cyanoacrylate

Cyanoacrylate, or instant glue, is another handy tool to have around. It's perfect for that desperate moment when you accidentally break off a fragile piece or chip out a chunk that should have stayed in place. Within moments of applying this substance, you're back in business. Try to stay away from the popular hardware store brands; they can be inferior in quality. Look instead for specialty brands found in woodworking stores, catalogs, or hobby shops.

Instant glue is also excellent for reinforcing an otherwise fragile area: simply apply the glue to the weak spot, and let it soak in. Within minutes the wood will be twice as strong as before.

A few words of caution: Cyanoacrylates are very volatile substances. The fumes will make your eyes and sinuses burn almost instantly, especially if you are bending over your work. Also, it will adhere anything to anything else, including your hand to the table. If you get stuck, don't panic. Applying pure acetone to the area should help, and a cyanoacrylate debonder is available at craft supply stores. The most important thing to remember is to peel away the co-joined areas; don't pull! Follow the instructions on the container. Wear gloves, a mask, and perhaps goggles, and use it in a well-ventilated area.

PAINTING AND FINISHING TECHNIQUES

Every carver seems to have a painting and finishing technique that he or she swears by. I have several that I like. The method I describe here has been applied to all the carvings shown in this book.

I use acrylic paints as opposed to oils because they dry faster and are easier to clean up. The cheap craft types in the 1-ounce (28g) plastic bottles are great to use. They are inexpensive, quality paints, and you can choose from a huge variety of colors, which virtually eliminates the need to mix colors. Because I am painting whimsical folk art animals, I choose creative colors that are not necessarily realistic. Use my choices as an example, but I encourage you to experiment with other colors as well. Remember: acrylics dry very fast (5 to 6 minutes), and they dry to a matte, not a glossy, finish.

Because you won't be spending much on paint, invest the money you saved in good brushes. I suggest a high-quality synthetic or sable brush. You will need at least three sizes:

> ½" (13mm) flat brush for blocking in colors
> ¼" (6mm) round brush for getting into corners and some detailing
> Very small round brush for detailing

Always clean your brushes well after each use, especially when using acrylics. Follow the manufacturers' instructions. Brush conditioners work very well and will increase the life of your brush.

Basic painting technique

The key to applying color that lets the wood show through, yet has depth, is to progressively layer it in thinned coats. This effect requires a few steps.

I first apply a thin layer of boiled linseed oil thinned to a 50/50 mix with mineral spirits to the entire carving. Boiled linseed oil and mineral spirits are available at most hardware, woodworking, and craft stores. Let it soak in for a bit, then wipe off the excess with a clean cotton rag. Let the carving sit overnight, or at least for a few hours. The application of oil helps to seal the carving, which allows different colors to blend together more smoothly; this preparation is essential for successful layering. Note: Be sure to wet your oil-soaked rags and dispose of them properly to avoid spontaneous combustion.

Any stiff brush with a straight edge can be used to stipple color on a painted surface.

Paint, using acrylic colors.

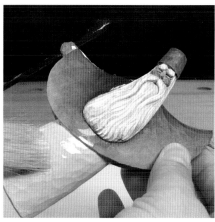

Seal, with satin polyurethane.

Finish, with brown gel wood stain.

THINNING. When applying the paint, have water on your brush as well as paint. I like to dip my brush in water, give it a shake, then load the brush with a dab of my chosen color. Apply it evenly, always keeping a wet edge on the surface of the carving while filling in an area with a single color. If you let the edge of a color dry then try to paint the same color next to it, you'll end up with a darker line of that color running through your painting.

LAYERING. Layering colors helps to give depth to the carving and improves the three-dimensional effect. Basically, you choose a base color for a given area. Then, use a darker hue of the same color for shadowed areas and crevices, blending it in with the base coat. In some cases, a lighter version may be desired for highlights. Just remember to keep each coat thin enough to see the wood through the paint.

WASHES. I sometimes create a wash from acrylic paints by watering a color down to the point where it acts as a translucent stain. In this case, I add a very small amount of the desired color to a paint dish of water and mix it in with a brush until the paint is evenly distributed. I then test it on a scrap piece of wood, adding a bit of color until I get the desired effect. The point of a wash is to achieve a tinted look, as opposed to a painted look.

STIPPLING. I used this technique quite a bit as I painted the ark. To stipple, you need an old ¼" (6mm) round brush that has seen better days. After a while, brushes tend to separate and spread out, no longer achieving a tapered point; this type of brush is perfect for stippling. You may even want to blunt the tip a bit more by trimming it with scissors.

When applying the paint, do not stroke, rather poke at the surface as if you were trying to puncture

it. To blend your stippled color into your background color, start with more of a wash for your first layer. Feather this layer out into the base layer, letting the brush go dry of color; continue to stipple for a nice transition of one color to the other. Now go back and strengthen your stippling color a bit by applying the second layer in the same fashion. The point here is to transition from one color to the other while creating an antiqued, blotchy effect.

Basic finishing technique

After the paint has dried for at least an hour, the carving must be sealed. This step is done for two reasons: to brighten the colors and, more importantly, to seal the carving for antiquing. If you skip this step and try to antique the carving without sealing it first, you will end up with a big mess.

Seal the carving with a high quality, fast-drying, satin polyurethane. Make sure you use satin, not gloss! It is important that you apply this finish as thinly as possible. I practically scrub it on with a disposable stain brush, working it into all the crevices.

Let the carving dry overnight. When dry, the piece should still look matte. A dull sheen is okay.

Basic antiquing technique

I like to antique my carvings. It pulls out the details and softens the pieces. To achieve this effect, I use an oil-based, gel wood stain. Oil-based gel is good for two reasons: First, if your polyurethane got a little too thick somewhere and left a shine, the stain will help

to dull that area a bit. Second, gel doesn't run. Whenever you use stain—gel or liquid—some excess always remains in the nooks and crannies. When left to dry, a liquid stain will eventually run out a bit and leave a little brown run mark. Gel stays put.

The color of the stain is up to you. I prefer to use anything titled "antique oak," "colonial," or "old oak." These colors appear to be dark brown but leave a warm, almost yellowed effect. Avoid "walnut" stains, as these are typically too dark to be attractive.

Apply the stain with a disposable brush, working it

into the deeper details. Slather it on! Then wipe it all off with a cotton rag. Make sure you do this immediately because gel stain dries quickly and you want the effect to be subtle. If you leave the gel on more than a minute, you will have a hard time getting it back off. I work quickly and usually apply the stain to the entire carving at once, but you may feel more comfortable doing these antiquing steps in sections.

Let the wiped-off carving dry overnight, and your carving is complete.

INDEX

ACQUISITION EDITOR
Peg Couch

COPY EDITORS
Paul Hambke and
Heather Stauffer

COVER AND LAYOUT DESIGNER
Jason Deller

COVER AND GALLERY PHOTOGRAPHER
Scott Kriner

DEVELOPMENTAL EDITOR
Ayleen Stellhorn

PROJECT EDITOR
Kerri Landis

PROOFREADER
Lynda Jo Runkle

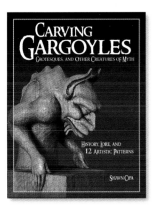

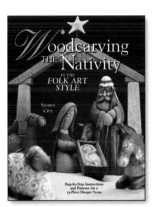
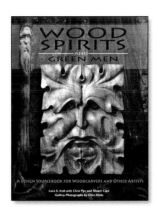

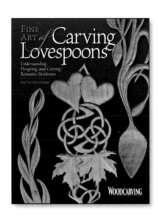